ROUTLEDGE LIBRARY EDITIONS:
HISTORIOGRAPHY

Volume 11

HISTORY AND HISTORICAL RESEARCH

HISTORY AND HISTORICAL RESEARCH

C. G. CRUMP

LONDON AND NEW YORK

First published in 1928 by George Routledge & Sons, Limited

This edition first published in 2016
by Routledge
2 Park Square, Milton Park, Abingdon, Oxon OX14 4RN

and by Routledge
711 Third Avenue, New York, NY 10017

Routledge is an imprint of the Taylor & Francis Group, an informa business

© 1928 C. G. Crump

All rights reserved. No part of this book may be reprinted or reproduced or utilised in any form or by any electronic, mechanical, or other means, now known or hereafter invented, including photocopying and recording, or in any information storage or retrieval system, without permission in writing from the publishers.

Trademark notice: Product or corporate names may be trademarks or registered trademarks, and are used only for identification and explanation without intent to infringe.

British Library Cataloguing in Publication Data
A catalogue record for this book is available from the British Library

ISBN: 978-1-138-99958-9 (Set)
ISBN: 978-1-315-63745-7 (Set) (ebk)
ISBN: 978-1-138-19548-6 (Volume 11) (hbk)
ISBN: 978-1-138-19555-4 (Volume 11) (pbk)
ISBN: 978-1-315-63833-1 (Volume 11) (ebk)

Publisher's Note
The publisher has gone to great lengths to ensure the quality of this reprint but points out that some imperfections in the original copies may be apparent.

Disclaimer
The publisher has made every effort to trace copyright holders and would welcome correspondence from those they have been unable to trace.

History and Historical Research

By

C. G. Crump

Author of *The Logic of History*, etc.

LONDON
GEORGE ROUTLEDGE & SONS, LIMITED
BROADWAY HOUSE 68-74 CARTER LANE, E.C.
1928

Printed in Guernsey C.I., British Isles, by the Star and Gazette Co., Ltd,

CONTENTS

		PAGE
	PREFACE	ix
I	THE ENQUIRING MIND	1
II	THE DISCOVERY OF A SUBJECT	35
III	THE SEARCH FOR MATERIAL	64
IV	NOTES AND THE MAKING OF THEM	117
V	THE FINAL STATEMENT	150

PREFACE

I BEGAN this book in the month of January, 1926. It grew in the first place out of a suggestion made to me by Professor A. P. Newton of the University of London; and at a later stage in its history it turned into the materials for some informal talks to a small number of graduate students, which at the suggestion of Professor Wallace Notestein I was allowed to give at Cornell University in the spring of 1927. On my return from that experience, in which I learned at least as much I taught, I rewrote a part of the manuscript in consequence of criticisms received from friends, who had been kind enough to read it and suggest amendments. Among them I owe most to Professor Becker of Cornell University, to the Rev. Claude Jenkins, the Librarian of Lambeth, and to Professor Newton and Professor Notestein, whom I have already mentioned. Their suggestions have improved the plan of the book and in places enriched the matter of it. I have also thank Mr. C. Johnson of the Public Record Office for help in avoiding errors. The faults of the book are my own; the friends who have helped me will, I hope, approve the use I have made of their suggestions, and pardon if I have misused them.

C. G. CRUMP.

October, 1927.

I

THE ENQUIRING MIND

THERE are many ways of writing a book and the merits of those different ways can only be determined by the taste of the reader and the discretion of the writer. But as a matter of convenience there is much to be said for a plan which puts the conclusion of the book in the first chapter. The reader will know at once what he may hope to find, the writer will know what he has to discover for himself and offer to the reader: what is even more important, both will get to know what the book is not meant to contain. This book, for instance, is not meant to contain any systematic account of the mechanical processes of the historian; it will not give any detailed instruction in the art of note-taking, or hints on the size or classification of slips; nor will it deal with the value of particular bibliographies or criticize the methods used by historians. Still less will it attempt to lay down canons of historical criticism or discuss the special difficulties that await those who wish to write on particular periods or subjects. Something may, indeed, be found on all these points, but they will only be discussed partially and by way of illustration of the main topic of the book, and that will be the case even in those chapters whose titles may seem to suggest that in them some systematic treatment of these matters is intended. The book, in fact, deals with one subject only, a subject easier to discuss because of its limitation, harder to define because there is about it a certain vagueness due to the manifold variations of the human mind. For it is the mind of the historical enquirer at which this book is aimed, his mental processes and his ways of thought; not indeed the mind of the accomplished scholar to whom inquiry has become a second nature, but the mind of the beginner, the tentative struggler, or even that of the worker who has never attained to any confidence in his own methods; one who like the writer himself is still wondering whether, like Lord Byron, he might not have done more, if his energies had been better or otherwise directed.

It has been said that there is a certain vagueness about this subject and that men's minds work in many ways. It follows that the reader will find here no prescription, no patent method, by which he can become an accomplished scholar; he will not even find a description of the typical mind of the ideal student. He will only find an account of certain ways of thought, certain intellectual processes, which the writer thinks he has discovered and admired in others, and which he would have liked to possesss himself. Moreover, he will find this account expressed, not as a whole, but in an apparently fragmentary form. He will find a discussion of the process of discovering a subject for study, another on the search for materials, a third on the process by which he may master those materials, and yet a fourth on the art of constructing a narrative. This method of treatment may lead the beginner to conclude that the author supposes that this order is the order in which historical work should be done, or that at any rate his mind is expected to think in that order. A careful reader may discover at intervals passages in all those chapters which will show him that the writer has no such belief. Lest, however, these indications should escape the attention of the reader, it may be well to point out once for all that no wise man ever worked in that manner, and that any student will soon find that all the four processes here described are so interlaced and so similar that he will inevitably find that he cannot find his subject without discovering and mastering materials at the same time, or do any of these three things without being able to express his results while he does them. Little by little it will dawn upon him that the ideal student's mind can do all these things together and yet know which of them he is doing at any given time. This last sentence is not far from being nonsense; it is only meant as a challenge to the reader to do better.

No doubt more than a mere challenge could have been attempted; but a writer is perhaps wise in refraining from doing more. The teacher who can use the actual contact of mind with mind may be able to enforce on his own pupils his own conception of the ideal habit of thought and way of work. The pupil, who is strong enough to profit by such instruction, will be the first to resent that intellectual domination and rebel against it; and the finest minds will always remember with gratitude the training which produced their eager revolt. Minds of less strength, incapable of rebellion, will not go far; to each of us character and intelligence, not to mention other factors, assign our limits. The methods of a teacher cannot be used by a writer. The teacher's control can be resisted only by rebellion; the writer can be restrained by the simpler method of closing his book. His first duty is to persuade the reader to refrain from this peremptory form of inattention. He must appeal to the reader's interest and remember that he is writing for unknown minds to whom he is himself unknown; and remember that dogmatic treatment of complicated matters is in itself repulsive. It would, for instance, be easy to begin this disquisition by advising all would-be researchers to practise the virtue of industry. From industry one could lightly turn to the praise of accuracy, and so to other virtues of equal importance. All these things are certainly needful to the researcher, as needful as are legs to a mountain climber or eyes to a greyhound. But by themselves they are useless. The object of this book is to discover the characteristic qualities which mark a certain habit of mind, and to that it is time to return.

No one who desires to do original work on history will begin his enquiry with a mind unformed. Methods of thought, ways of approaching a subject, convictions, dislikes and admirations, susceptibilities of interest and boredom will already be in existence and more or less powerful. Some of these habits of mind will be known to the student, others will make themselves felt by degrees, and some will only be apparent to his friends and critics. Taken together they make up the character of the individual mind, either original in it or acquired. A student need not trouble himself about these facts or try to alter them. All he has to do is to know them, so far as he can, to know where he is likely to be led astray by his mental character, and where he may let himself advance with safety.

This is not a work on mind-training and is not intended to start anyone on a futile search for self-knowledge. Yet it is necessary to point out that every mental process, every acquisition of new knowledge involves the use of a mechanism of thought and memory already trained by use and experience to take a particular view of facts submitted to them. Now it is often suggested that the student should aim at freeing himself from these fetters and endeavour to attain an *intelligence déliée,* and that only by such an effort can he become that impartial spectator of the past who alone has the right to call himself an historian. No one will dispute the magnificence of the ideal, but it is permissible to doubt whether even those who praise it most eloquently ever attain to it, or even know how much the impartial man must forfeit in his pursuit of that splendid virtue. In the first place he must surrender all desire to take a side in the controversies of the past, and study to conceal his own view of them, even if he dares to have one. He must judge, for impartiality means judging; he must therefore be able to award a due measure of praise and blame to the great men who struggled for the rival ideals which have distracted mankind. To do this he must understand the motives of the most diverse characters, and without adopting either side give judgement on the merits of the case. He must decide between St Dominic and the heretics whom he quelled, between Frederick the Second and the Popes with whom he contended, between Boniface the Ninth and Philip the Fair, between Leo the Tenth and Luther; on the intellectual side he must be able to assign their rightful places to St Bernard and to Abelard, and settle authoritatively the vexed question of the right of the clergy to temporal wealth. If we turn to modern times the impartial historian will have to settle the measure of blame or praise that should attach to Philip the Second of Spain; Elizabeth, Richelieu, Mazarin, Charles the First, Strafford, and Cromwell must pass under his judgement. He must appreciate Burke and Wellington, explain Napoleon and know the inmost soul of Bismarck. Nor is this all; he must fit himself to pass impartial sentence on the great movements, which draw men into the sudden fits of energy which disturb the even course of history; he must estimate the good and evil of revolutions, balance the harm of wars against their benefits, and know the motives which cause men to leave their homes to seek prosperity in strange lands. He must make his own code of law, and while he applies it can know neither affection nor dislike for the men or causes summoned before his tribunal.

He may, of course, repudiate the responsibility[1].

[1] For Ranke's view, see note at end of this chapter.

He may say that it is not the business of an historian to be a judge, and that the question of impartiality does not arise. His business is to understand the actions and the motives of Napoleon, for instance, and express and explain them; nor need he consider or pronounce judgement upon the righteousness or even the wisdom of them. That is the duty of the reader, if indeed it is the duty of any one. That by this course the historian avoids many difficulties, is clear enough; and yet even in this way of work there are perils to encounter. In the first place such a writer must definitely avoid one part of history; the history of the development of ethical ideas. He must not say that the shooting of the Duke of Enghien was a crime or even a blunder on Napoleon's part. He must merely describe the mental state of Napoleon which led him to order the arrest, the trial, and the execution of the man whom he desired to put out of his way. In the same way he must deal with such matters as the massacre of St Bartholomew or the persecution of the Quakers in New England. He will have to watch his style very carefully, for one of two things is likely enough to happen to him as he writes. His language will become cold, colourless and even timid, or he will become a master of irony; and the man who becomes a master of irony too often, like Gibbon, is mastered by it in the end. Nor is this the only peril to be encountered; the worker may slip into the belief that a scientific[1] method of study may enable him to attain 'objectivity'; that he can passively observe and discover facts and present them to the reader exactly as he receives them without allowing his own mind to affect the accuracy or character of the presentation in any way. Language is a difficult tool, and has its own ways of disconcerting such a scheme; and the words that come from a writer's pen have an awkward way of defying all attempts at objectivity by expressing the subjectivity of their selecter without his knowledge. Probably the recording angel is the only example of an historian who is both impartial and objective. Again it might be urged that in the pursuit of these qualities it is easy to go too far; it would be easy to discover believers in democracy who in their zeal for democracy blindly praise Napoleon, who was not a democrat; while others, zealous supporters of authority condemn the one man, who above all others knew the value of authority, and wrecked his cause by over-insistence on it.

One thing is at least clear. Even those who believe that impartiality and objectivity are duties incumbent upon historians, must admit that they are

---

[1] Anyone who thinks that scientific method can exclude personal peculiarities should consider the meaning of the 'personal equation'. An Astronomer Royal, some generations back, is said to have dismissed an assistant for carelessness because his observations of the time of transit of stars across the meridian of Greenwich always differed by a constant quantity from those of the Astronomer Royal himself.

not easy duties. Minds capable of this task are few; only those can work in those high places who can endure solitude. Only those can attain to them who have been fortified by long study and strengthened by participation in great events. For minds not so equipped the pursuit of these qualities is an adventure too high. Let anyone who doubts this, make a list of those historians to whom he would allow these merits without qualification. No such list will be attempted here. But it is easy to mention names which have no claim to be placed in it; Gibbon, Voltaire, Michelet, Macaulay, Carlyle, Mommsen, Treitschke. All are great names, and many more could be added. Nor would it be difficult to give a list of great historians who have tried the adventure and failed, or only succeeded by writing history without considering the passions of the men who lived among the events of which they write. Yet these men too have written great works. But it is the men in the first list who command the attention of their readers and their words still live. Yet if any of them had tried to write impartially or objectively, that very effort would have silenced them. The very fact that they have a definite point of view to maintain inspired them and attracts the reader whether he agrees with them or is provoked to dissent.

The beginner, who aims at impartiality and objectivity, will assuredly hamper himself and fail to achieve them; it is far better for him to put all such ideals on one side, and let his mind work freely on its own natural lines. Let him take lower levels and train himself to be an advocate before he attempts to play the part of the recording angel. To do this he must possess the virtues of an advocate[1], including above all the virtues of fairness and honesty. The task of passing final judgement he may leave to those who essay it, and to the advocates of the other side. It is his part to practise honesty and fearlessness in expressing such opinions as he may form or possess; and for this purpose he will do well to observe two rules of conduct. The first rule is that the evidence for all conclusions must be stated as it exists in the source from which it is taken, avoiding any method of statement that may alter or impair its meaning or its emphasis. The second rule is that the writer must distinguish clearly between the evidence and any criticisms or inferences made by himself. These seem simple matters, but like most rules of conduct they are simple to state and hard to obey. Yet no one can be an honest advocate who does not observe them. The temptations to be dishonest are at least twofold. The first temptation is that of the partisan; over that there is no reason to linger. The beginner need only recognize that being human he probably is a partisan

[1] It is the old academic rule that the candidate for a degree must 'maintain his thesis', *i.e.*, he must be the advocate for the position he takes up. He must have a position or a cause to defend.

and that for that very reason he must practise honesty. The second temptation is more subtle; it is the temptation that assails the investigator. It is hard to part with the neat point, the promising discovery, the new light directed on some dark and disputed corner of history, just because some troublesome document, some new interpretation turns up to disprove the conclusion that the student has reached after long inquiry. There is always the chance that more research might set up the shattered theory once more; and more research may be impossible. His only safety lies in the rule of honesty; he must neither suppress the new evidence nor pretend that it is immaterial. He is entitled, if he thinks it wise, to maintain his position, to act as an honest advocate. He may weigh the conflicting evidence and decide that the weight of evidence is on his side. Such a decision, however, lays on him the duty of stating his own position with the utmost precision and of setting out the facts that tell against him with equal clearness. When he has done this, he will be wise to consider whether he may not be in danger of incurring the reproach that he has wasted skill and energy on a hopeless enterprise.

It might be supposed that the duty of being an honest advocate could be discharged more easily if the subject avoided controversial subjects. It might also be suggested that at first such subjects should be avoided. It is no doubt true that some subjects[1] provoke the worst passions of historians more easily than others. But it is not only in such subjects that temptations lie. One man may find it easy to discuss fairly and temperately the relations between Elizabeth and Mary, Queen of Scots, or the policy of England during the American Civil War, and have difficulty in dealing honestly and courteously with those who object to his ingenious explanation of the origin of an obscure document or scorn his emendation of a corrupt text. No one can say where or how controversy may arise; and though no one is bound to seek controversy, it is useless to attempt to avoid it. Indeed no advocate can become an efficient advocate who does not learn to enjoy it within the limits of wisdom and courtesy. By controversy the honest advocate learns to state his own case in its clearest and most attractive form and gets from his opponent the best assistance in giving the same clear and attractive form to the case against him. If, then, he can find no antagonist to help him, he must enter into controversy with himself, and test in that way the honesty of his study and the clearness of his results.

In our attempt to construct a model of the mind

[1] In some countries at some periods it has been the case that it is almost impossible and even dangerous for an historian to attempt to discuss certain subjects. The influence of political passion on the writing of history is worth study. An autocratic or a democratic government seems equally ready to censor opinion, though the methods employed differ. Countries may still be found where such things happen. It is difficult to find ones in which they do not.

of a researcher we have now come to the qualities most difficult to describe, in fact it may well turn out that they are undescribable. A good many words suggest themselves at once, some of which are often used, such as imagination, ingenuity, the use of a full mind, and so on. All these represent more or less accurately a very needful quality for which no adequate word seems to exist. The quality in question is in fact not easy to describe. The first condition for its existence is a well-stocked mind, a considerable body of knowledge. It is not, however, enough to have acquired this body of knowledge; it is necessary to possess it, to be able to use it and to find in it the particular thing needed. It is necessary to be able to deal with one's own knowledge as a student deals with his own library, in which he can without difficulty take down any book because he knows instinctively where it lies on the shelves. Some people call this power memory and consider that the power of producing knowledge at call is a proof of a good memory. It is rather the result of a dexterous and practised memory, attained because its owner has taken pleasure in continually turning over and examining the contents of his mind until he knows his way about it. This knowledge can, of course, be obtained in other ways. Some men have a delight in systematic thought; in their minds each new piece of knowledge has an appropriate place ready for it, carefully linked up with the others to which it is related. Facts no longer needed, discarded theories, are swept away, and the whole content of the mind falls into an orderly and accessible form. The possessors of this type of memory have their own reward; that they also have their own disabilities may appear later. The other type of mind is a trouble and an anxiety to its possessor. He knows many things; he has forgotten how he knows them. Nothing that he has ever known is discarded, no theory, however exploded, is cast aside. Instead of an orderly and classified collection of facts and theories, a sort of mental museum and card-index combined, his mind resembles a rag-bag into which its owner has put all his property valuable or worthless, tattered or whole. And this heterogeneous collection he must continually turn over and go through if he is to retain any control over it. These are the two extremes; between them may be placed all the intermediate types; and we must always bear in mind that all minds have their own methods of order and disorder.

Is there anything to be said that may console the owner of a disorderly mind, when enviously and ruefully he watches the serene course of his fellow student who is a systematic thinker? In order to answer this question it is necessary to get some idea of the possible methods of arranging historical events in the mind. The simplest method is of course that based upon an ordered series of events; and the most obvious order to choose is the order of time. Upon this conception is founded the ordinary device of historic charts, much praised by many authorities and quite interesting to construct. We have all seen the long bands of paper marked off by vertical lines into equal divisions of time with the various historical events shown by other lines. Sometimes they are plain, sometimes coloured, so that each colour represents a different geographical or national unit. An invasion or migration can be marked by the spread of one colour into the space of another. The result of a war can be shown by heightening the tint of the conqueror and reducing that of the conquered; and a period of confusion can be admirably represented by a display of intermingled tints resembling the result of an explosion in a dye-factory. The constructor of such a diagram will find much scope for ingenuity in his task, and may learn something. As a mind-picture of history, and it is with mind-pictures we are dealing, it is useless and even misleading. No mind, not even the most encyclopædic can possibly store in such a manner all the facts it needs to have at its disposal. Nor can any such arrangement represent with any accuracy the turbulent passage of events. As soon as the constructor of such diagrams endeavours to become an enquirer or a discoverer, he will find that his whole system of events ordered in time and space has very little to do with historical research or discovery at all. It is in fact only the elements of the whole matter; and such an arrangement of events or indeed any other arrangement is about as useful to a historian as a dictionary is to a poet. The poet must have the words; the historian must have the events; but neither can use them except in an order and relation devised by themselves.

It is precisely at this point that all methods of storing events in the mind fail; any method, in fact, presupposes that historical events stand in a definite relation to each other and can be arranged in accordance with that relation. In truth only the student himself who is making his collection of events for a particular purpose knows the relations he wishes to impose on them; and the more experience he has, the readier he will be to admit and insist on the right of anyone to use any historical events in any relation that may seem likely to be useful. Any arrangement that impedes the mental alertness required for such action is for that very reason to be avoided. The mind must be free to experiment, to notice that the battle of Leuthen was fought on the same plan as that of Leuctra or to speculate on the possibility that the victories of Salamanca and Poitiers were due to the same error in the tactics of the defeated generals. Any one who wants to attain to this alertness of mind must learn to deal in relations rather than in isolated events, and be ready to form as many theories as may be needed for this purpose and be even readier to abandon them when they have served their purpose. The student works in the main by noticing new relations between known events, and using these new relations to suggest the possible existence of unknown events.

It will be noticed that no attempt has been made here to define any of the terms used, and that in particular both event and relation are left undefined. The reader who complains of this shameless neglect may be invited to try his own hand at defining an event, and when he has performed that feat, he may go on to define a relation. In the process he will have built up a theory of causation, have escaped the jaws of innumerable man-traps, and acquired a skill in dialectic which in these days will probably be of little use to him. For the purpose of this book, which is not a treatise on logic, philosophy or psychology, it is only necessary to point out that every student of history ought to know an event when he meets it, and that he also ought to know that every historical event can be analysed into as many other events as may be found needful for the purpose of more detailed discussion. The degree of analysis is a question of convenience, settled by the particular purpose for which the event is used. For some purposes the French Revolution may properly be termed one event; for other purposes such a use of the term would be an absurdity. In the same way the relations between events are of the most varied kind. Some may depend on the closest connexion in time or space; other relations may depend neither on time nor on geographical unity, but merely on the fact that at all times and in all places things of the same kind are apt to happen in the same manner. Nor can we exclude certain relations which perhaps only exist in the mind of the enquirer, who is led by his own habit of thought to link together certain events for reasons peculiar to himself. The important thing is that every researcher should acquire the habit of constructing a net-work of relations between all the events known to him. He must be ready and curious in inventing and devising new ways of looking at familiar things, and keep his mind flexible and his critical judgement active.

It is now possible to see how the two types of mind described above will approach this task. The systematic mind will have its stock of events ready to hand, accessible and critically known. Its disability will lie in the very fact that the discovery of new relations involves the disturbance of the familiar order so carefully achieved. All the stored events must be turned out and sorted and re-sorted until the neatness and tidiness of the old arrangement has disappeared. The old habit of order will of course resist this process; it will seem to involve a loss of accuracy, the substitution of vagueness for clearness, an attempt to replace knowledge by mere 'viewiness.' Now turn for a moment to the possessor of the disorderly mind. His habit of mind has forced him to be continually turning over his stock of events; he has been compelled in sheer self defence to establish all sorts of queer devices to keep his knowledge in any kind of control. Flexibility of mind, the invention of odd clues to the labyrinth of history are second nature to him. Events of the most diverse kind lie side by side in his memory without shocking him; accidental juxtaposition is always a possible source of new views to him. The very consciousness of his own lack of systematic order has taught him to be at any rate critical if not honest. One thing he lacks, and must acquire, the power to impose order when order is needed, the power not only to know things but to know how he has come to know them. Just as the owner of the systematic mind must acquire the power to break up the array of his ordered knowledge, so the owner of the disorderly mind must try to introduce some neatness into the disorder in which he keeps the events he remembers. No doubt, as the reader will note, these extreme cases are, like all extreme cases, imaginary. No minds are completely orderly; few are in complete disorder. The normal mind probably lies nearer, a good deal nearer, to the disorderly type than to the orderly. At the same time it is the case that it is true that most students think that the latter type is the right thing to aim at, the type to admire and envy; and many critics and teachers share this view. And yet though the luckless possessor of an untidy mind is always conscious of his own sins and filled with respect for the supposed possessor of a tidy mind, in his heart he knows very well that he gets far more fun out of his work than the other fellow, and thinks, possibly with some justification, that he finds out more things, even though he makes more blunders.

There are fortunate minds that are both orderly and flexible, minds which can pass rapidly and easily from one system to another, and know at any moment the system best suited to the task before them; these can see the events of history as a whole and impose upon them any order desired, and discover the relations between the most widely separated times and places. They have their reward and need no advice. All that less fortunate students can desire of them is that they should reveal their power in their writings, and occasionally let us see their way of work and not only the results they attain. Perhaps that is the one power denied to them; it is not always possible for the eagle to explain his way of flight or his power of vision.

But the faculty of mind here discussed does not lie

only in this power of detecting relations between events. There is another side to it, the power of seeing events as they happen, of constructing what I have elsewhere[1] spoken of as the drama of a particular event, a theory of the way in which that particular thing must have happened. At first sight it may seem that this is a task only to be performed by means of careful enquiry into all the accessible material bearing upon the point. If this were the case, the drama so constructed would be the same thing as a finished treatise on the subject, and no special use of imagination or dexterity of mind would be needed. The real meaning of this power of dramatization is different; by its aid the enquirer can take any event and form a mental picture for the way in which it took place, can expand it by placing it among the other events with which it must have been connected, and analyse it by showing all the sub-ordinate events which lie within it[2]. For the materials to do this the worker should be able to rely on his accumulated store of facts and in particular on his knowledge of how things happen. He should be able to dispense with

[1] *The Logic of History* (Helps to the Study of History), S.P.C.K., p. 52.
[2] One of the most amusing experiments in this way of working, though it does not deal with an historical event, may be found on p. 44 of a little book called *Sermo Latinus,* by Professor Postgate. In this passage the author by a judicious use of imagination has expanded the brief statement that " Balbus was building a wall " into a full and probable account of the character and motives of Balbus, the nature and magnitude of the wall, and its architecture, and the result of its construction.

any materials, except perhaps a date or so, and a glance at one or two books of reference. His aim should be to test his skill in seeing through the screen which any brief statement of an event raises between him and its real nature, and to destroy the illusion that when he has stated an event he knows it.

Any event might be taken as a starting point for such an exercise. In fact the student will do well to apply the method freely in his work. The example which will be given here is only one of many which might be given. It is chosen as a simple case, and some of the process may seem trivial; but it has the advantage that the very fact of its simplicity makes it easier to follow every step. Let us begin with the event, which event of course was noticed in a written form. In the year 1909 any traveller in Rome might have happened to start on the following walk. He might have started from the bottom of the Via Cavour, the new street which runs from the Forum up the base of the Viminal hill. When he got near to the church of San Pietro in Vincoli he would naturally turn to the right up some steps and come into the open place in front of the church. He would, like a good traveller, turn into the church and look at the tomb of Julius II and the statue of Moses carved by Michael Angelo with the famous knee. In this walk his historical imagination should have been raised to its keenest pitch. He will have left behind him the monuments of the great days of Rome. He will have passed near the place where Tullia the wife of Tarquin is said to have driven her chariot over her father's body; and near to the terrible dungeon with its memories of the deaths of Jugurtha, Catiline, and Vercingotrix and its story of the imprisonment of St Peter. He will have seen the tomb of the mighty Pope who drove the French from Italy and quelled the genius of Caesar Borgia. He will be in a mood to see history behind events. From the place before the church there runs down hill towards the Coliseum a street called the Via della Polveria, the street of the Powder Magazine. On the left hand side of that street there was in 1909 a long wall covered with stucco, coloured a soft pink. There is nothing in the street of any interest except this wall, and the only interesting thing about this wall is that there was in it a large arched door-way, large enough to admit a cart. It was closed by a pair of rickety doors which were once painted green. Over the arch was an inscription recording an event. It is not likely to be there now; the hand of the builder will have destroyed wall, arch and inscription together, without heeding its importance or interest. But in 1909 it could be read without difficulty and it ran: "*Empire Française. Depôt de Poudres et de Saltpêtres.*"

At some time or other there was then in Rome a powder magazine and a store of salt-petre belonging to the French Empire. The first impression on any one who read this inscription would be one of surprise that such a notice should have been allowed to remain for every passer-by to read. In 1909 there was no French Empire and the Government of Italy would not have readily accepted any claim from the French Republic to possess a powder magazine in Rome. It would soon appear that the letters had been put there many years before 1909 and had stayed there simply because no one had ever troubled to have them removed. The first step in constructing a theory of this event would naturally be to fix a date at which the scribe, who made the record of it, set up his ladder and his scaffolding, and after consulting his instructions painted the inscription above the doorway. Little if any help in dating the inscription could be got from the character of the lettering, nor indeed would such methods, though invaluable in dealing with early inscriptions, be needed in this case. A first hasty conjecture might lead the enquirer to dig out of his store of facts the presence of a French force in Rome for a period ending in 1870, coupled with a hazy recollection of Garibaldi and Mentana. But the form of the inscription would stand in the way of this theory. It distinctly suggested that the French Empire was the dominant authority in Rome. Moreover the street was called the street of the powder magazine; the name must have come from the magazine and be older than the inscription; the magazine must have been put there by the Papal government; the inscription must record an act by which the French Empire took over the Papal store of munitions and with it the whole government of Rome, and with Rome the whole of the Papal Territory. From his store of facts the enquirer would pull out the dates 1809 to 1814 and the whole drama would begin to grow up in his mind. Before he went further, another hazy recollection would come to his aid. This was a store for salt-petre, not only for gunpowder. The inscription went back to the days when all belligerents had to look to their supplies of salt-petre. There was trouble in France over salt-petre in the days of the directory, when the supply from India was cut off by the English fleet. The great chemists of France found a way to solve the question. The search for salt-petre was carried on in old houses,[1] cattle-byres, and the mud floors of such places, the dirtier the better, were made to yield up their store of nitrogen and ammonia. Some book on agricultural chemistry would tell the whole story. Anyhow Rome and the country round Rome would have been a good field for searches of the kind. It all fitted in with the date of 1809.

And so the whole story—the imagined story—

[1] This seems to have been a half recollection of some process connected with the scraping of stucco from old walls. There would have been plenty of that round Rome.

began to grow; first of all the slow penetration into the states of the Church by Napoleon's troops. Murat seemed a likely guess as the leader of the occupation, done of course under the most careful screen of due form. Murat[1] would have been in the neighbourhood, he had played a like part in the seizure of Madrid in 1808. At any rate, until one knew, he would do for a symbol. Under him and with full instructions from Napoleon the process would be sure. There would be a period of encroachment; a puzzled Pope knowing that sooner or later he would have to do something, not quite sure when to do it, or what to do. Finally Napoleon would have taken some resolution and told Murat to act, and force the Pope to carry out the policy, which Napoleon required him to adopt. The Pope was to submit to the imperial system or disappear. The exact questions at stake must be left over—to be discovered later if ever. Murat would have assuredly bettered his instructions. The Pope would have snatched at his professional weapons, and promulgated a bull with a fine beginning, say, "Patrimonium Petri".[2] The Spanish precedent would have been remembered; Murat would have seized Rome, arrested the Holy Father, sent him off a prisoner, and annexed the city, the patrimony of

---

[1] Murat was a good guess, and Murat had a big part in the play. The actual agent was, however, General Miollis.

[2] It did begin "Quam memoranda". The guess was naturally a bad one.

Peter and the powder magazine and in due course the painter would have set up his ladder and recorded this part of the transaction in the inscription, which the traveller might have seen still in existence in 1909 just a hundred years later. This of course need not have been the end of the traveller's speculations. He might have gone much further, and constructed a picture of the sort of resistance, which the French occupation would have provoked; he might have guessed that the clerical body in the Papal States would at any rate have begun a passive resistance, and carried it to great lengths; and guessed that there would have been some support for the new government among those who had resented the exclusively clerical government of the Papal States. The organization of the country into departments might even have attracted his attention. He did well, I think, to stop where he did. The whole constructed drama grew out of an inscription containing eight words; the edifice based upon it was perhaps a little top-heavy, and in parts rather inclined to totter. To go further would have needed more knowledge and more material. As it is, there is plenty to correct in the drama, and much to add to it. Two points have been mentioned in which the guesses made were wrong or only half right. But any student who knows the facts or cares to look them up will be able to discover plenty of faults in the story. Nevertheless, any historical enquirer will, perhaps after some hesitation, agree that some such process does represent the first stage in historical thinking.

Nor is this all that could be said. It is a process that must be employed at all stages of any investigation Each new fact or event that is taken into the mind ought to be made the starting point of a similar process, and the construction of such dramas should be a habit of any enquiring mind. There is of course a danger to be noted and avoided, the danger of falling into a habit of fantastic speculation and lack of concentration and consequent waste of effort. The attempted guess at the title of the Pope's bull in the drama given above is a good specimen of that kind of folly, a folly which needs to be checked as soon as it is noticed. A student's imagination is not the proper place in which to look for such details; and in the specimen here given there are too many details. The construction of a drama should not be allowed to outstrip the known facts too far. It should be carried far enough to make sure that the worker really knows the nature and strength of the facts he knows, and far enough to suggest to him the places where he needs further material for new speculation. The ultimate limit depends on the purpose he has in mind, on the article or book he means to write. From this purpose he should not let himself be distracted by the ease and fascination of the process. If any beginner should here object that though the process may be fascinating, it is not fair to call it easy, there is one reply that may be made. Those, who do not find it easy, will find all historical investigation difficult and irksome; or, as is often the case, on reflection they will find that they have been using this method in some form or other without knowing it. "No one possesses living knowledge of any history except as it is imaged in some fashion"[1], and it is living knowledge which the enquirer desires to have for himself and to impart to others.

Within the limits here suggested the value of the method is clear enough. By constructing such a drama the enquirer lays down the main lines of his investigation of any event. How far he will pursue them, depends of course on the purpose for which he means to use his knowledge. In any case he knows where he is; discovers the extent of his ignorance and is forced to examine and re-arrange the contents of his mind. Nor is this all; by such exercises he will attain a clearer vision of the realities of history, and cease to satisfy himself with the definite phrases which are so easy to use, and which so often conceal the real way in which things happen. He will gain a sense of the importance of the unknown facts of history. Such terms as 'The Renaissance', 'The Reformation', 'The Industrial Revolution', and the like will seem

---

[1] I owe this sentence to Professor Becker of Cornell University.

to any one, who thinks in this way, to be little more than brief head-lines, or short titles, which reveal nothing and are apt to conceal everything worth knowing about the events they purport to describe. He will be reluctant to use historical documents without considering how they were drawn up and the materials that lie behind them. He will acquire the art of criticism, and the habit of discovering relations between events, and using these relations to suggest the existence of events unknown, and materials hitherto unused. Nor is it only substantives that need this treatment; effective as substantives can be in misleading or preventing thought, adjectives are even more ingenious in deceit. 'A constitutional king', 'representative government', 'a strong monarchy', 'democratic institutions', 'a patriotic people' —the list goes on indefinitely. But translate all these adjectives into action, and then check the adjectives by the results of that process; they will look different after it. Some will lose the tarnish that familiarity has brought upon them, and take on a new polish; some will lose any meaning that they ever possessed; and some will acquire a completely new meaning, which they never had before. All will have been tested, will have ceased to be mere tokens; the student will have a living image in his mind, and know whether he understands the words he uses or not. Most important advantage of all he will have to some extent discovered the extent of his ignorance and the limits of his knowledge.

The example of the method given above is a simple one. It would have been just as easy, if not easier for the writer, to deal in the same way with a larger and more complicated event, such as the conclusion of the treaty of Westphalia. But the drama of such an event would have been longer and perhaps duller to read, and the simpler case was chosen as an act of mercy. No one is likely to suppose that the writer has any claim to possess any but the most general knowledge of the events of the year 1809. And this may serve to show the beginner how easy it is to construct such a drama without special knowledge.

It is now possible to state the results of this enquiry into the mental attitude and ways of thought, which a beginner should desire to possess, a beginner that is, who is not inclined to class himself with those who are entitled to be a law unto themselves, able to pursue their own path alone, guided by the lamp of their own genius. He need not aim at impartiality or objectivity or hamper himself with a fear lest his mind should suffer from bias. All that he need aim at is courage in maintaining his positions and honesty in stating his own arguments and those that tell against him. He must have as large a store of events and relations as he can acquire and remember that on the whole he should be anxious to keep his mind flexible rather than orderly. He should practise the art of 'dramatizing' his events, so that he may test his knowledge and his ignorance and escape from the illusions produced by phrases half understood, and acquire a habit of criticism and clear expression. There are other qualities needed of course. But with these the beginner may be content. They will at any rate help him to recognize, if not to escape, the great enemy that lies in wait for all historians to-day, the enemy who call himself 'scientific method' and whose true name is 'meritorious dullness'.

With this we may end this account of the mind of the beginner, who has determined to devote at any rate a portion of his days to historical research, and means to enjoy that curious way of life.

Note to page 7.

This seems to be the meaning of Ranke's famous sentence in his preface to his *Geschichte der romanischen und germanischen Völker von 1494 bis 1514,* published in October, 1824, and (3rd edition) reissued in 1874. The sentence runs: "To history has been assigned the office of judging the past, of instructing the present for the profit of the future; such high offices this essay claims not for itself; it merely shows how things really were." Those who read German have a right to the original words: "Man hat der Historie das Amt, die Vergangenheit zu richten, die Mitwelt zum Nutzen zukunftiger Jahre zu belehren, beigemessen; so hoher Aemter unterwindet sich gegenwärtiger Versuch nicht; et will blos zeigen wie es eigentlich gewesen." But a little lower we find: "Strenge Darstellung der Thatsache, wie bedingt und unschön sie auch sei, ist ohne Zweifel das oberste Gesetz." This is not an easy sentence to translate, but it may be paraphrased, as follows: "A rigorous statement of facts, even if this course results in an incomplete and awkward narrative, is the first law for the historian." Ranke's own writing in this very book shows that a rigorous statement of fact can hardly be made without judging and even condemning individuals and nations alike. A statement of fact is often the most effective form of judgement. In any case Ranke's "course few sons of men may dare to emulate." See also *Cambridge Modern History*, vol. xii, pp. 824 *sqq.* for a discussion of this introduction and the controversy that sprang from it (by C. P. Gooch).

There is much more that may be said upon Ranke's view of history; and many better qualified to say it than the writer of this note.

II

THE DISCOVERY OF A SUBJECT

THE main object of this chapter is to set forth some of the methods which the beginner may use to discover the subject which he desires to make his own. Before, however, this exposition can be attempted it is necessary to set out certain axioms which will be assumed in that discussion and to note some dangers to be avoided. These axioms, like all axioms, will be self-evident and the warnings will seem superfluous. In spite of this neither the writer nor the reader of this book can escape from the necessity of the task of considering them, and consideration may show that they are not so obvious or superfluous as they may appear at first sight.

The axioms are concerned with the general nature of a subject proper for historical treatment in the form of a monograph. No attempt will be made to construct any definition of the terms subject or monograph; all that will be done is to mention the marks that must be looked for by those who are in search of these elusive things. If from the study of these marks, the reader can frame a definition he will be more fortunate than the writer has been. Now the first axiom is that the subject must be one that can be treated in a monograph, or in other words it must be possible to isolate it and exhibit it as a separate whole apart from the main body of history. Sometimes this quality will exist naturally in the subject, sometimes it will be necessary to introduce it more or less violently; but it must be emphasized that the best subjects require the least violence. The next axiom is that the subject must possess historical value; the work that is to be done on it must not be wasted on material of little value. The result of the work done must be designed to fill a definite place in the structure of relations and events which make up the whole of history. Moreover, this place must be vacant or at least incorrectly or imperfectly filled. And so we come to the third axiom: the subject must possess the quality of novelty. It must be so chosen as to compel the worker to make discoveries and to add to the sum of historical knowledge, either by pointing out new events and relations or by a novelty of treatment which will exhibit events and relations already known in a new light. Finally we come to the last axiom; the subject must suggest questions that can be answered. There must be material, existing and accessible, on

THE DISCOVERY OF A SUBJECT 37

which the study of the subject can be founded. This last axiom does not strictly belong to the present chapter; its place comes later in the book, but it is included here because it is assumed in the discussion that follows.

After the axioms come the warnings. Do not choose for a monograph a vague and confused subject which like Dr Parr's wig expands " into a boundless convexity of fuzz ". Make sure that it can be reduced to a manageable and definite form. Do not waste work on trivial and unimportant matters or be led aside into mere technicalities. Such work has to be done, but it is not work for a beginner. Only wide knowledge and great experience can fit a man to tackle minute questions of detail with ease and certainty and enable him to display their relation to a general scheme. It may be well that someone should spend time and energy in discovering why the marriage between William the Conqueror and Matilda was irregular or in examining the menu of the meal set before Napoleon after Marengo; but these are not subjects important in themselves. Avoid hackneyed and fashionable subjects; it is difficult to annex to your own dominion things that are common to all. Finally do not endeavour to discover " the name Achilles bore among women ", not only because it does not matter whether we know it or not, but because there is no material that can enable any one to arrive at it. The fact that the answer to a question is unknown is no proof that it can be discovered.

One last warning must be added. There is a curious and pestilent idea abroad that the first duty of a student is to register the title that will be placed at the head of his monograph. In consequence the student on the track of a subject begins by formulating a brief description of it in which he will aim at a nicety of style, recalling the brevity and point of an epigram. He may even go further and invent the title of his monograph, when he can have only the vaguest notion of what it is to contain. Some of these titles seem almost machine-made. A student will have a fancy for political philosophy and a knowledge of economic history, and announce that he proposes to write on the " Political Ideas of the Industrial Revolution ". Or he may seek for a legal subject and propose to discuss " Theories of Criminal Law among the Early Quakers ". Titles like these—both are purely imaginary—can be turned out wholesale; they require little thought and not much knowledge. But they are only titles, not descriptions of subjects, and should be avoided like all other spectres. In other words do not be in a hurry to formulate your subject, still less to find a title for it.

Dogma has its own use, and a little of it must be pardoned by any reader, even when the writer protests that he only sets down his fundamental axioms constrained by a sense of duty, conscious that these axioms represent precepts not practice, and that any reader of this book will be able to use these pages as means to convict him of inconsistency. With a cheerful sense of one more duty accomplished, we may now return to easier matter. The first chapter discussed the habit of mind which the beginner should endeavour to acquire. This chapter may reasonably contain an examination of the beginner himself, and also an apology for the use of the word at all. For by this term the writer means not those students, who are mastering the relation between King Alfred and flapjacks, nor even those more advanced who can accurately reckon up the number of the wives of Henry VIII, but those really accomplished students who have read history for themselves or under accredited guides, and know, if not much, yet many things. Certainly the man who has successfully accomplished a course of study at an university and more than satisfied his examiners, may fairly complain that he has been subjected to an unmerited dose of cold water if he is told that he is now just ready to begin the serious study of his subject. Perhaps reflection may do something to convince him that no reproach is meant by this hard saying, and that it is in fact a pleasant truth. He has already done much; he has learnt many things and been taught more. He has obtained a general view of the whole of his subject, has collected a stock of facts and learnt how to add to his stock. He has had practice in dealing with printed materials, collected and arranged for his use; and, if he is lucky, he has acquired a body of knowledge and a method of critical thought, which will serve him well throughout his life. If he finds on reflection that he is not disposed or not qualified to make serious contributions to historical knowledge, he need not regret the labour he has expended. Perhaps as he watches the toil of those of his fellows who enter on a course of historical research, he may even murmur in the words of the saint: " Alta scrutantibus deus paravit gehennam."

But for those, who are minded to take that path, these words have no warning. They will go forward on their high adventure, resolved to meet all difficulties, and rejoicing in the anticipation of their labours. They will not lack encouragement and assistance; indeed they will sometimes meet with a superfluity of both. Those are both wise and fortunate who remember that the first test of the fitness of a student to undertake research is to be found in his power to work alone, supplying his own stimulus, planning his own course of action. No one who knows the doubts that assail the student engaged on his first enquiry, the difficulties that bewilder him, will under-estimate the value of intellectual sympathy and of common discussion of problems with others engaged in like work; and more will be said on this

THE DISCOVERY OF A SUBJECT

point hereafter. No one, however, can fail to know the danger of the research " limited to the Degree and the Dissertation " and particularly of " the research commanded by the Professor, and got up by the pupil just well enough to pass ", of which Professor W. P. Ker[1] spoke with regret. The first duty of the student is to insist on taking his own line; the first duty of the professor is to see that he does so. The old relation of teacher and pupil must be broken down and a new relation created between them, a relation of equality, of common endeavour, of mutual criticism. Especially should the student keep strictly in his own hands the control of his first and most important step, the choice of his subject. The student who is compelled to ask his teacher to suggest a subject to him, and the teacher who accepts the task, are equally in error; and the error is least excusable in the student, for such a lack of resource shows that he is deficient in one important quality, the power to think alone. He is not yet anxious to be quit of control, has not put off the attitude of a subordinated mind and become a free man.

Both student and teacher have to consider how to set up this new relation between them, and it would be absurd not to admit that it may be a painful task. Old habits of mind, old bonds of loyalty may have to be broken, and in some cases the difficulty is best

[1] *Collected Essays of W. P. Ker*, vol. i, p. 149.

met by separation. The student is in fact often well advised if he goes to a fresh university; the professor is wise if he insists on such a course. And even where this is neither possible nor prudent a temporary separation is commendable. Until the student has found his own line of work he should avoid or evade instruction. It may be said that the students who can make such a selection are few in number; that the majority have no experience of research, cannot know what materials exist for the discussion of a particular question or how far it is capable of treatment, and have no chance to discover whether its novelty is not exhausted by works already published or about to be published by experienced writers. All this is true; these are points which every student has to consider, objections that may be made to his choice. He is fully entitled to ask and receive any information that he may need on such matters. But the final decision rests with him. He may have to alter or even abandon the subject he has chosen, and admit that he has not given sufficient thought to his task, and has lacked the skill and knowledge needed for his purpose. At any rate his failure will have taught him one thing, that the choice of a subject is not an easy task. It may even have begun to be clear to him that subjects are not chosen by researchers, but that subjects choose the researchers. This saying, like most paradoxes, needs explanation.

THE DISCOVERY OF A SUBJECT

Any man, who has a rational desire to be eaten by a lion, will find that it is needful to leave the civilized parts of the world and go into deserted and waste places. If he has also the refined intention of being the first man to be eaten by that particular lion, he must choose places to which men rarely go, or where at any rate they tarry only for a brief time in a hasty passage. For the same reason a student who desires to be found by a subject, a new subject, must go where subjects live, and make his habitation in that area. The first step is to choose the area. All time and all the surface of the earth is open to him. From any date at which he may believe that history begins down to any date at which he supposes history to end he may select any piece of the earth's surface as a likely spot where his subject lurks ready to seize him. His choice of an area must depend on his taste and on his knowledge, and should not be difficult[1]. The only warning that need be given is to look first at his weapons. The first weapon to examine is the stock of languages. Travelling in a country where the language is unknown is a sad experience, and the study of Byzantine history is hardly possible to those who know no Greek. Of course there are not a few historical students who are well equipped and there are

[1] If the student finds his choice difficult he can easily obtain advice from others. But by the time a student has done enough work on general history to be fit to begin research he ought to know the regions and the periods which interest him.

others who know enough of some languages to be able to learn more quickly. These need no warning; but there are others who may be more adventurous than wise; and it may be well to tell such that it is little use for them to plunge into medieval research unless they can read Latin fluently and accurately or can afford the time to acquire that power. If the survey of his weapons, convinces the enquirer that he knows the languages in use in his chosen area, he can proceed to a further examination of his resources, and consider whether he can read the writing there used. If he doubts this point, he need not therefore abandon his purpose. A man, who knows a language, can learn to read writing with great rapidity and without serious difficulty in all normal cases. He may start for his chosen area without fear; by his own efforts with the assistance of good instruction, he will easily master this detail without great delay. But effort and instruction will both be needful if this part of his armoury is to be in good order, and he must always remember that at any moment he may meet with writing that is not normal, and fall into serious error if his training does not enable him to recognize the danger. The only other requisite is that he should have a good general knowledge of his chosen area, such a knowledge as any historian would have, who has looked into that part of history. If he has more, so much the better, but as usual enough is enough.

Once he is satisfied that he possesses this modest equipment, his course is open to him. Let him seek his area and settle down in it, and expect his subject. Let him examine everything curiously and critically, books, documents, calendars, lists, catalogues, antiquities and so on; let him at the same time talk and discuss if his taste lies that way, or ponder and reflect if he prefers silence to speech. Anything that he comes across that he knows already, he will soon begin to see in a new light; he will take pleasure in inverting his dogmas and standing his established facts upon their heads. The things he has never known will become precious to him; and difficulties and unintelligible passages in the books or documents he reads will be his dearest discoveries. A note on the margin of a letter or an account, a figure on the back of a deed will start him in pursuit of a new enquiry. And sooner or later, if his mind is ready and of the right temper, from some bundle of rolls or from the page of some book, the lurking subject will leap upon him and claim him as its prey. From that moment his difficulty will lie not in finding a subject but in escaping from it.

Πολλαὶ μόρφαι τῶν δαιμονίων, as Euripides tells us at the end of more than one play. There are many shapes of inspiration. Nor is the method here described the only road open to a student. A fortunate mind may be inspired to discover " a point in Hamlet's soul untouched by Germans yet ", or a still wiser mind may have found in his schooldays a subject for the exercise of his matured abilities. These fortunate men may be left to their own happy guidance; they need no advice. It may, however, be said that for less fortunate men the course advised here means much waste of time. Can the student afford to embark on the sort of miscellaneous reading here suggested? In particular is it not ridiculous to commend such practices to those in search of higher degrees at some university, who only intend to complete the academic exercises required for such degrees, who only desire to be masters and doctors and regard the composition of a thesis[1] as a means to that end? The answer to this question is not an easy one. It would be absurd to deny that this class of students exists. It would be even more absurd to deny that many of them, if not most, need all the assistance that can be given them, and is given them, in the choice of a subject and the composition of a thesis. It is also true that many of these produce " results laboriously acquired and useful "[2] to themselves if not to others. They deserve the degrees which they receive, and have doubtless added to their store of knowledge.

[1] The pronunciation of this word is uncertain. In some universities the first syllable is made to rhyme with mess; in others it is pronounced to rhyme with grease. The first pronunciation should only be employed by students who know Greek. The second is good enough for those who only know English. Compare Dr Parr on the pronunciation of Alexandria.

[2] *Collected Essays of W. P. Ker,* vol. i, p. 149.

THE DISCOVERY OF A SUBJECT

But it would have been far better for all of them had they at least tried to work alone, and only fallen back on the aid of their teachers when experience had convinced them that they lacked the power to choose for themselves. The time would not have been wasted; they would at least have learnt how to handle evidence, how to find books and documents, how to read and interpret them, even if they lacked the power to see the subject waiting for them in its lair, ready to pounce upon its appropriate prey.

Nor is it necessary to deny that in some cases the suggested subject, the carefully supervised research, the manufactured thesis, may result in producing a trained researcher; even a trained researcher who could have been created in no other way. For exceptional minds exceptional methods are needed. All that is meant here, is that for most of that small body of men who wish to practise research, the way here described will be found the best, the best both for teacher and student; for the teacher because he will know that the student has been taught to do his own work, for the student because he will have the sense of adventure and the knowledge that success is all his own, and that for failure he need reproach no one.

After this explanation and apology we may return to the point at which we left the student. He has chosen his area, made his habitation in it, taking with him suitable equipment, and has encountered his subject. It is possible that in its first shape the subject may not meet his requirements exactly. Indeed it is almost certain that it will fail to do so in one important point; it will be too large and will require to be limited in extent and made definite in meaning. In order to effect this limitation in his subject, the student will be well advised to consider his own limitations. The chief of these is naturally the limitation in time. How many years is he able or willing to devote to his first research? The regulations of most universities allow him two or three years for the task, and though these periods are intended as a minimum limit, university students are naturally compelled to treat them as a maximum. Fortunate students may, of course, fix their own limits; but even for them it is best to choose a subject limited in extent. Every beginner needs time, time to waste, time to devote to exploring blind alleys, time to give to subsidiary points that will demand attention, time to collect all the information he must carefully acquire and as carefully refrain from setting forth in his finished work. Above all the beginner needs time to escape from the domination of his subject, to lift his eyes from the fixed contemplation of his narrow field of research, and survey the surrounding country. He must keep time in hand to master and understand the background that lies behind and around his contemplated work.

THE DISCOVERY OF A SUBJECT 49

The limitation of time implies the limitation of the size of the subject. Now, as has already been said, and it cannot be said too often, men's minds work in many ways. Some workers, especially the least experienced, begin by choosing a large subject, and then narrow it down to a practicable size by a process of exclusion. They will valiantly contemplate a work on the history of international finance under the Plantagenets, and finally produce a monograph on the relations between a particular king and one firm of Italian bankers. The more experienced worker is apt to start from the other end. He will begin with a small point, a trivial incident, a difficult sentence in one document, even a marginal note, and let his research grow from that point, knowing well that he will have no difficulty in expanding his subject, though he may find it hard to keep it within bounds. Both methods have their advantages. The beginner, who uses the first way, will be compelled to survey a wide tract of history in order to select the small part of it, which he can treat in detail. He will thus be saved from the danger of dealing only with an isolated piece of history, while ignoring its relation to the main stream of events. The other way can indeed only be followed effectively by those who, either by experience or by that fortunate tact which supplies the lack of experience, can discern the needed point of departure for their enquiry. No one can be advised to choose this way; but no one should be deterred from following it if he desires to run the risk of taking it. The risk is clear; it lies in the probability that the small point, the discovered difficulty, will suddenly disappear, and on investigation turn out to be susceptible of some trivial or even absurd explanation. Mr Jonathan Oldbuck's discovery of a Roman inscription on the Kaim of Kinprunes is a familiar instance of such a disappointment. Nor is that distinguished antiquary the only researcher who has experienced such sorrows. For obvious reasons only those who suffer in this way know their own woe; the tale of disillusionment is not often told publicly. On the other hand the rewards are great. The successful investigator of a small fact, which grows into a large discovery, has the joy of feeling that he has attained something in an irregular, if not illicit, manner. He has also the joy of the prospector, who "strikes it rich," and values his gold the more that it has come to him partly by luck and not entirely by reasoned effort.

Let us leave him to his satisfaction; and turn to the strict path of logical advance, the first way, the discovery of a large subject which must be limited by a process of exclusion. The chief reason for this necessity, the question of time, has already been discussed. But there are many other reasons which deserve mention. The principal one of these is the

THE DISCOVERY OF A SUBJECT

limited skill of the beginner. The larger the subject is, the larger is the mass of material that must be gone through, and the greater the temptation to collect notes and references. Any investigator, at any rate any conscientious investigator, can collect more notes in six months than he can use in six years. However methodical he may be, though his cards be like the rainbow in their coloured glory, though his classification be perfect and his cross-references impeccable, sooner or later he will find that he does not really know what he has got in his notes; he may even discover to his shame that he has made the same note twice over, or that he cannot be sure in what part of his collection a particular and precious reference lies concealed. These are the troubles of the beginner, the sorrows of the first enquiry. But if he will recognize betimes the danger, and measure his task by his skill, his sufferings will be less and his results better. A limited subject means, in fact, a limited mass of material and a limited number of notes; and a limited number of notes means that they can all be kept in the memory, so that the task of writing out the results of the research will be the easier.

Again the beginner is usually, though not always, unskilled in writing. Even if he likes to write and does it well, the composition of a lengthy work is a strain on his powers, and may mean a heavy demand on his time and on the patience of his readers. It is one of the duties of any writer to present his results in a clear and, as far as possible, in an agreeable form. A limited subject makes a short statement possible. It is unwise to suggest any definite number of words. This book and its author lack the courage required for such an enterprise; neither dare say more than that most academic theses, first theses that is, could profitably be reduced by a quarter of their length; and that there are few important works setting forth the results of historical research that do not contain superfluous pages. Meiosis may be suspected by the cunning reader at this point, but it is only fair to warn the cunning reader against entertaining unworthy suspicions.

It will be remembered that the subject was originally discovered by selecting an area for investigation and inhabiting it. It might seem possible to limit the subject by a somewhat similar method, and it might even be supposed that the task would be an easier one. It seems that this is not the case; the discovery within a large subject of the special part suited for a limited research is apparently a difficult and delicate task. Now in an earlier part of this section the professor was warned, perhaps with too little ceremony, that the selection of a subject was a matter for the student alone, and that his assistance in that task ought neither to be offered or desired.

THE DISCOVERY OF A SUBJECT

But here it seems proper to warn the student that there is a point at which he will do well to return from his solitary expedition to the academic fold, in search not of assistance but of criticism, of criticism given by the more experienced worker and given the more trenchantly and keenly because it is criticism given in the form of discussion between equals. Such criticism and discussion is the best help a student can have at this point; it will test his knowledge of the possibilities of the subject, show him how to remove the unnecessary portions of it, and bring out and emphasize its most important lines. Moreover, in the course of such talks the student may get an idea of the impression made on his critic by his choice, and correct any misconceptions into which he may have fallen. Nor need he despair of getting hints as to materials, printed and manuscript, and other valuable advice; he may even have the pleasure of murmuring as he leaves an interview, that he had already found out some of these things by his own unaided efforts. Some professors, even the most critical, have no great objection to being told as much, if the information is judiciously conveyed to them, always remembering, "male si palpas, recalcitrat undique tutor."

The limitation of the subject can be effected in other ways, and indeed other methods must be employed in addition to that of submission to professional criticism, and even before that method can properly be tried. The first step will have been taken when the student has got a clear idea of the class of the subject on which his choice has fallen, and is thus able to mark off the essential and main thread of his search from its subordinate parts. Now all classifications are imperfect and misleading, but all are also useful within the limits of common sense and sanity. There is no harm in dividing up history into *Political History,* the history of States, of men as political animals; *Economic and Social History,* the history of men as producing and consuming animals and their success and failure in both capacities; *Legal History,* the history of the law under which men live: *Administrative History,* the history of the way in which governments and individuals manage their affairs, and the *History of Civilization* (or 'Kulturgeschichte'), which discusses the influence upon human beings of their art, literature, philosophy, religion, and ethics. There is no harm in this classification, so long as it is used and not misused. A closer examination of the various classes will reveal some of the dangers which await those who misuse these divisions. We need only consider one case, e.g., *Legal History;* the same criticism will apply to all other classes, *mutatis mutandis.* A research into a question of legal history may be of two kinds at least. It may be a research into the origin and history of legal principles expressed in the judgments of qualified courts of law or in legislation or of a doctrine discussed by lawyers in books of authority; or again it may start with political or social conditions or changes and examine the results of these changes on the law prevailing in the society in which they occur. No one would embark on a research of the second kind without paying careful attention to the facts of political, social, and economic history. On the other hand it would be quite possible to begin a research of the first kind, on such a subject as "Early examples of the law of contract in England", and forget entirely two considerations of some importance. It would be easy to forget that all law is produced and enforced by the society in which it prevails, and that in a sense the law of a society is founded upon the form of that society. A developed law of contract implies an individualistic theory of society; and in a completely socialistic community no law of contract could exist at all, since every contract would have the state as one party and every breach of contract would be a criminal offence. Accordingly every research into law must be based upon a knowledge of social forms and conditions. The other important point is this; no court of law, save in very rare cases, will decide a point until that point has been raised in a case brought before it; and it will often happen that a long growth of opinion has to take place, before any litigant or lawyer will think it profitable to raise a new point of law in a case to be decided. Legal history is often the history of a doctrine that has lagged behind opinion and even behind practice, and this delay produces curious results. A lawyer writing on law for lawyers must use terms and theories that may be quite unreal. Sir William Blackstone must write of the land law of England in terms of feudal tenures, in spite of the fact that in his day feudal tenure in England had ceased to exist as a real fact for some centuries. In the same way a conveyance of land, until very lately at any rate, would contain in its operative clause the word 'to hold', as though no ownership but only a tenure was in contemplation. And here again the researcher who relies solely on legal cases and law books may easily be led into writing good law and bad history. His only corrective will be in his knowledge of those classes of history which lie outside his strict subject. Sometimes an even more complicated error occurs. A lawyer in court finds he has a bad case, meritorious in ideal justice but bad in law. He has to do his best for his client, and the whole of his ingenuity is needed. In such a case everything, argument, citation of precedents, historical truth, and even sense may be cast aside from sheer necessity. In some cases both sides and the court itself may lose their way in the fog of difficulties; and so leave to the enquirer who is endeavouring to discover, e.g., the answer to

THE DISCOVERY OF A SUBJECT

some conundrum in constitutional law, only a maze of ingenuities, which have no real value as the expression of what men of the time really thought was the law, still less of what they thought was the theoretical basis of the law. Here again the only chance of escape lies in the power of the researcher to check one class of historical evidence by his knowledge of other classes.

So it is with all the classes described above. They are all interwoven and inter-related. To study successfully any one of them the others must be kept in mind. A change in an administrative process may be due to a political change or to an alteration in the economic condition of a country. An alteration in the economic condition of a country may lie at the back of a change in opinion on questions of religion or politics; and yet such a change may take place and its results may be concealed by the natural inertia of men's minds, which will cling to established institutions and accepted opinions long after they have become inapplicable to the new conditions of life. In the case of law the importance of this 'lag' in time has already been noted, and the same factor is of equal importance in all the other classes listed above. It is one of the reasons which make it difficult to express history properly in terms of causation; since even if we confine causation to mere succession in time, it is hard to be sure that we have really ascertained the true order of the events which we arrange as a chain of causes.

All these considerations must be borne in mind by the student who proposes to limit his subject by taking into consideration one class of historical events and excluding the others from his survey. Some classification, indeed, is a necessary step and a powerful aid to any writer. It must be made, but it will not be necessarily or even preferably the classification already given. Here again the student must claim and assert his own independence and make his own definitions. The stock classes, the traditional limitations, are the enemies of discovery, the destroyers of original thought. The valuable part of the process of classification lies in the necessity of defining the subject, and the best classification is the one that exacts the clearest definition. But just because it is the right and duty of a student to construct his own definitions, there is not much that can or ought to be said here on this point. All that can be done is to provide a few warnings. These are only warnings, not prohibitions; no intellectual adventurer should fail to disregard them without hesitation. The first warning is this: do not hastily use the obvious definitions founded on time and space. It sounds so easy to define a subject as "Constitutional Doctrine in the Lancastrian period in England" or "The Use of Allegory in the Literature of the Thirteenth Century in Provence ".[1] Both these titles assume that there was something special about the use of allegory or constitutional doctrine at the place and time mentioned. This proposition may be true and in that case the definition may be a good one; it may be false and in that case the definition is bad. The danger, and it is a real one, lies in the fact that the student may fail to consider whether the assumption in his title is founded on fact or not. He may too easily fail to see that his definition merely amounts to cutting out an arbitrary ' chunk ' of time and space, and may go yet further into error and end by assuming the existence of some real peculiarity there and then, simply because his choice suggests that it must be so. At this point the reader may be asked to look back to the words in which the warning was given and notice the use of the word ' hastily '. It is only the hasty student who need fall into this error. The cautious and thoughtful enquirer will know the danger and keep his eyes wide open as he works. He may finally change his titles and produce a useful monograph called: " Did any New Constitutional Doctrines come into Existence in the Lancastrian Period in England? ", or " Is the Use of Allegory peculiar to Literature of the Thirteenth Century in Provence? " He may, in fact, come to resemble the probably mythical hero

[1] It may be objected that this is not History but Literature. None of the subjects discussed in this book are to be taken as suitable for historical research.

who invented a perpetual motion, went to the University of Cambridge to study mathematics to perfect it, and become a senior wrangler. The fate of the perpetual motion machine remains unknown to mankind.

Another warning may also be given; do not hastily assume that the subject cannot be defined in space or time. Often this is the most effective method of limitation. No objection can be taken even to an arbitrary definition of this kind, provided that the definition is stated to be an artificial method of selecting a portion of a large subject, and that the intention is to use the limitation merely to enable the researcher to study in detail a small portion of a great series of events. Such a subject as " The History of the Wars of the Roses in the County of Rutland " may be a good choice, provided that there were any events worth examining within that area. Nor could any objection be taken to an attempt to write in minute detail " The History of Agrarian Movements in Little Pedlington from the Ninth to the Nineteenth Centuries ". But in either case the writer would have to be careful to use his limited investigations in such a manner as to relate them to the events of general history. And so we reach naturally the final warning, already hinted at in this chapter. Remember that, when once your subject has found you, your difficulty will lie in escaping from it.

The danger lies in the fact that the very definition and limitation of the subject may blind the student; he may become incapable of seeing anything but his subject. He will refuse to look beyond the lines he has himself drawn round it, and begin to regard his classification as expressing an historical fact instead of an imaginary line drawn for his own convenience. Buried in his subject, he may forget all others. The last few sentences contain metaphors enough to impress the warnings on the most careless reader. It is hardly necessary to enforce it in more words. Nor is there any need to insist on the fact that the absorption of the student in his subject is a virtue, since it is a virtue dear to the heart of any enthusiast. It is so pleasant to accumulate notes all dealing with one neatly defined topic, so easy to reject all information that seems impertinent or beside the point, so delightful to follow the narrow way that leads straight to the goal, so virtuous to avoid the wide discursive route that leads to the wasting of energy in acquiring a stock of miscellaneous information. All this is true and there is no need to impress the truth on the student who knows it already. But let him remember to keep open ways of escape; in default of these he will find that when he comes to write down the results of his research he will be producing something that he can barely endure to write, and that no one but an examiner will think of reading. The examiner has no choice; anything that is laid before him he must read. It is even possible that in a state of coma he may mistake dullness for profundity, and fancy that an interesting piece of writing must be unsound.

There is only one thing more to be said, and that is a thing that has been said already, but must be said once more. The researcher, if he is to do original work, must regard research as an adventure and enjoy his work. He must insist on his right to work alone, and in particular to choose his subject himself. It is his adventure. But if he is to enjoy it to the full, he must dwell among those engaged on like adventures. The most delightful part of a scholar's life is the time reserved by him for meeting and talking with other scholars. Best of course are the talks where a few like-minded students are gathered together, and mutual criticism is allowed full play, meetings arising without premeditation or ceremony. But almost as good may be the organized meetings at fixed times and places, where some expert *primus inter pares,* a man strong to keep silence himself and to induce speech in others, can gather beginners about him, and send each of them away feeling cleverer and wiser than they did before they entered the room, with a sense that all they have contributed to the general fund of talk has come back to them clearer and sharper because they have themselves said it and heard the comments of others upon it. The enjoyment of research lies in sharing its results; the work of research is a solitary adventure, and like all solitary adventures is a mingled experience of glorious achievement and resolute failures.

III

THE SEARCH FOR MATERIALS

THE attentive reader will have noticed that in the last chapter one grave question was passed over somewhat delicately. The materials for research were only mentioned and were indeed treated as things known to everybody and accessible to all. It was, indeed, suggested that a knowledge of the languages in which materials were written was advisable, and that the student would have to possess or acquire the power to read the manuscripts which he proposed to employ. But beyond these observations the matter was left in obscurity. In this chapter it is proposed to attempt a closer study of a very complicated question. Logically it falls into two neat divisions, the discovery of materials and the use of them. Like most neat divisions this classification fails in practice; it fails for the simple reason that each process involves the other. The student cannot begin by making a complete collection of his materials and then sit down

THE SEARCH FOR MATERIALS 65

to find out how to use them, for the obvious reason that without this knowledge he cannot be sure that he has chosen the right materials to collect. Further it is clear enough that he cannot learn to use materials unless he has materials to use. Both processes, in short, must go on together. Still, as we must begin somewhere, we may as well begin with a consideration of the art of discovering and collecting materials, leaving to a later chapter the discussion of the method of employing them. It may, however, be as well to warn the reader that it will not be possible to keep the two subjects apart, and that chance only will decide under which head a particular topic may be found.

In order to deal with the whole class of materials it must, of course, be divided. It might seem best to found these divisions upon the nature of the information to be obtained from the several classes. If this were done, the student who had chosen a particular subject could then turn to the following pages with a confident expectation that he would find in them a clear and definite account arranged in chronological order of the materials to be examined, their place of deposit, the hours at which he could consult them, the best routes by which to reach the towns containing them, with advice on the proper hotels, and a few pages on the method of placating crusty custodians. There are only two reasons against adopting this course. The first of these is that the writer shrinks from the task of compiling a book in more than one volume, and that the proposed scheme, if thoroughly carried out, might require sixteen. The second reason is that it may fairly be doubted whether such a book, even when done, would be any great use to a beginner. Certainly it could not possibly enable any student to ascertain in what places he would discover all the materials he needed for a particular research. The very fact that the student is going to undertake such an enquiry, presupposes that he means to know more about it than any one else does; and for this purpose he must get an equally exceptional knowledge of the materials from which he means to obtain that knowledge. He must know the materials that any expert will know; but beyond that he must find the materials very few experts will think of suggesting as a likely source of information. Experts who are only experts, have, in fact, certain limitations. The width and accuracy of their knowledge renders them overconfident; the fact that they know where information can be had, and where it ought to be had, sometimes may lead them to think that they know where it cannot be had. Yet this is knowledge that no one ought to claim to possess. No one can be sure that any class of materials cannot be used for some purpose of which previous investigators have never thought; and it is in fact the mark of a good searcher that he can find what he wants in places where others have never thought of looking or have looked in vain. For these reasons, among others, the writer respectfully declines to tell beginners where they will find materials appropriate to their purposed research; and some sad experiences of his own make him unwilling to tell them where they will not find such material. *Semel insanivimus omnes;* but no one need act like a lunatic more than twice.

But, though we set aside any attempt to compile an exact and complete guide to historical material, much remains that can and ought to be discussed here. The general nature and proper classification of material, the main classes and the sub-classes into which it may be divided, are matters very proper to be here considered; and we may set about it either logically or practically. There are good reasons for taking either course; but lest the reader should feel a sudden surprise and even turn away from the book as a gourmet might leave a dinner which did not begin with a proper *consommé* and go on with a *sole meunière,* we will begin with a taste of logic. All material may be divided into two classes, primary sources and secondary sources. Primary sources are those sources which give the first information attainable of the fact or event to be discovered. Behind them it is impossible to go, so far of course as the student knows; they are the source of the stream of information, the point at which authority ceases and conjecture begins. Secondary sources on the other hand are those which are derived from primary sources which are either known to exist or are discoverable. Logic is always a useful weapon to employ, even if, as sometimes happens, it burn the user's fingers like a red hot poker accidentally picked up by the wrong end. But it is a weapon with limitations; it is useful for criticism rather than for discovery, and in this chapter it is intended to consider discovery first and leave criticism for later discussion. But a little thought will show the reader that the application of this inexpugnable means of division to particular cases is likely to demand the most delicate and ingenious study and will often lead to controversy rather than to certainty. One instance may suffice; let the beginner consider the task of constructing a pedigree of the manuscripts of a particular book, e.g., of the *Divina Commedia* of Dante, or of Bracton's treatise *De Legibus Angliæ*. How far will the distinction between primary and secondary sources help him there? And in the study of any historical question and of the sources available for its solution, the same or similar questions will arise at every stage. The truth is that this distinction, well known as it is, is really a fact to be discovered by methods of criticism and should always be treated as such.

Let us therefore abandon logic for the present and turn to practical methods. The first thing needful is some sort of division based on methods of access, on the kind of places in which material exists, and on the shape it takes. The readiest method is to think in terms of printed books and manuscripts. Printed books suggest libraries; manuscripts suggest archives, record offices, private or public, and museums. Like all rough and ready classifications the distinction is imperfect, but the awkward cases are chiefly matters for amusing discussion. It is not necessary to linger here over the question of the exact place to be assigned in this classification to a cinema film or a collection of pictures or photographs. The logical discussion of these questions may well be engrossing; here we will simply point out that in practice such points do not trouble the researcher, however much anxiety they may reasonably cause to professional keepers of archives and museums. For the beginner the important point is that he should begin to think of his material in terms of the places in which it exists; and this because the people who describe historical material, especially unprinted material, use that method; and they use it because the place of deposit is an important point in the history of all manuscript material and of certain printed material. It is enough to mention here the obvious fact that the place in which a reader finds such a book as Chamberlain's *Description of England* for a particular year is not likely to be of historical importance, while the occurence in a particular place of a rare pamphlet may often be worth noting. Apart from rare cases of the latter kind the place of deposit of a printed book is unimportant; the problem of access to such material is in most cases easy to solve, and the discovery of the book required only needs a certain measure of knowledge. Moreover, in his first course of study the student will have already acquired much knowledge of books and a power of discovering and using them. We shall therefore first treat of printed material.

The chief point to be dealt with here is not such elementary matters as the nature of libraries or even the use of bibliographies. It is rather the acquisition of a new mental attitude towards printed material. It has already been pointed out that the intention of a researcher is to discover historical events and relations hitherto unknown. In consequence he is now far more concerned with the things that are not mentioned in the books he reads than with the things there described fully and accurately. Definite additions to knowledge based on adequate evidence are merely material to be considered in one of two ways; if such things are known to the reader, he will pass lightly on; if they are unknown, he will carefully add them to his store, especially if they are relevant to his subject. What he must look for are the points passed over lightly and incompletely, the places where accessible material known to him was clearly unknown to the author, the too hasty theory founded on error or ignorance, the gap in the argument, the brilliant generalization which veils imperfect knowledge. It is not the merits of the book that he must linger over, but its weak points and above all its omissions. Especially is this sort of reading needful in the first stage of a research, the stage in which the reader is looking for his subject or hoping that his subject will find him. It is in the weaker parts of books that subjects are apt to lurk. For this kind of reading the particular book chosen for study is of far less importance than might be supposed. Of course the best books must be read; but just because they are the best books, they are likely to contain the fewest opportunities for new enquiry. The scholarly author, master of his subject, equipped with all past knowledge and all contemporary literature, who has read all that has been written and checked his knowledge of printed sources by the study of unprinted material, has two grave faults. His authority imposes on the reader, particularly on the novice; he can build an apparently solid edifice out of shaky materials on an unsound foundation, and do it so well that neither he himself or his reader will ever doubt its security; or if he prefer another course, he can hide his ignorances from himself and from his reader so cunningly that neither shall ever discover them. That is his first defect as a suggester of subjects for research; the second is that it is ill to go gleaning where he has harvested; the field is apt to be bare. Sometimes, indeed, but not often, an author may be found to say: " This question, important as it is, I cannot answer; this difficulty I must leave to others to solve." But even here there is little comfort for the beginner; these questions, these difficulties are for the most part beyond his power to attempt. Sometimes one almost seems to detect a hope in the writer's mind that his challenge may always remain unanswered, the knot he points to never be untied. But all the same the best books must be read, and perhaps even in those unlikely coverts the game may be started.

But apart from the disadvantages noted above, the student who confines his attention to the best and latest books loses one source of inspiration. He has not watched the growth of knowledge or studied the tradition of error. The study of these processes is enlightening and enlivening and fertile in suggestion. There is no better method of acquiring the power of using books than to take a received doctrine and trace it from book to book, noting how it developed into its most recent form from its earliest appearance in print. It is tempting to mention some promising points for such an enquiry, but the reader of this book has been told so clearly that he must find his subjects for himself that I lack the courage to disobey my own edict. But no student will ever regret the time spent in such

THE SEARCH FOR MATERIALS 73

pursuits. He will have learnt much that he can learn in no other way; he will have learned to respect the scholars of by-gone days and have won the power to appreciate men like Selden, Dugdale, Madox and their fellows; or in another field he may come upon great works like those of Ducange or Père Anselme, or Mabillon, and he may even find out the use of dictionaries like those of Bayle or Moréri. He will find in them or through them the origins alike of truth and of error. He may become familiar with Coke and through him with Littleton and so pass on to Sir William Blackstone[1] and come at last to Tidd, beloved of Uriah Heep, in whose pages he may find the solution of not a few riddles of legal procedure, if such matters interest him. It is not a question of reading these and other such books, but a question of knowing how to use them, though no one interested in law can fail to feel the charm of Blackstone's work at any rate, even if he fail to appreciate the arid genius of Tidd. It may seem to the hasty reader that he is being advised to look at odd books. If indeed he takes this list as an authoritative guide to legal history, he will certainly have a right to think himself misled. Let him remember that this list is not a list of books or even of authors; least of all is it a guide to the study of law. It is put here simply to illustrate the wealth

[1] I mean of course Blackstone as Blackstone wrote it, not as edited in later times. Never look at a modern edition of a legal classic, except for legal purposes.

of old books that exist as sources of knowledge and the names are simply the first names that drop from the writer's pen. They happen to be chiefly lawbooks, but that is only an accident. A similar list might have been given on other topics. One might, for instance, have taken general or political history, and set down a chain of authors from Matthew Paris to Hallam, or from Clarendon to Hume and on to Carlyle, although Carlyle's *Cromwell* still survives when Hume's *History of England* has died. One curious fact will emerge from these books, the origin of the received characters of historic persons; these characters are as traditional as the characters assigned to animals in the school books of the last generation. The cat is "treacherous" for the same reason that Henry the Seventh is "sagacious"; because some author assigned that character to each, a Bestiary perhaps to the cat, Bacon certainly to the King. Even the origin of certain technical descriptions of historical events is a fair subject for enquiry; and not only the origin, but also the change in interpretation, which results from use, and the reasons for that change. Is it, for instance, the case that we speak of the Black Death because it is called by that name in Mrs Markham's *History of England*? Who first used the phrase 'The Peasants' Revolt'? and who summed up the economic change, which produced the manufacturing system of the nineteenth century, as 'The

Industrial Revolution'? If we mean to use such terms intelligently we must know their origin and how their inventors used them. Without such knowledge we shall soon be involved in a game of Russian scandal, and end by using such phrases in a sense which those who invented them would have repudiated, or even in a form which their authors never used. We shall come to speak of the principle of *laissez faire,* not knowing that we are using only half the sentence, and that half in a sense which the inventor of it never contemplated. There is but one remedy for this mental disease, and that remedy lies in discovering the origin and history of such phrases before making use of them.

So far the argument has dealt with books in general and with the proper method of regarding them. But this is only the beginning of the subject and the next question to be considered is more complicated. It is, in fact, absolutely necessary to consider the selection and arrangement of the books needed for a chosen subject. Until the subject has been found these considerations are unimportant, and nearly all the remarks hitherto made apply to that period of study when the student and his subject have not yet succeeded in meeting. But when once that stage is past the mere consideration of time suggests that some order and limitation must be introduced into the books which the student intends to read.

The limitation means selection, selection means experience, and experience is exactly the quality which the beginner lacks or is most likely to lack. No doubt there are bibliographies to be had, many bibliographies, large bibliographies, classified bibliographies, special bibliographies; there are also catalogues of libraries, ranging in size from the catalogue of the library of the British Museum down to the smallest book that ever called itself a catalogue. There are even bibliographies of bibliographies, and it is not improbable that sooner or later some enterprising university has already found it necessary to establish a diploma in 'Bibliographology', with a Reader attached. Assuredly something of the kind will soon be needed for the guidance of the inexpert student through the maze which the efforts of enthusiasts are preparing for him. But interesting and useful as bibliographies can be, especially to the makers of them, they all have one grave defect. They are most useful to those who need them least. If a student knows the names and the value of more than half the books that he ought to consult, bibliographies may help him to conjecture what other books he ought to add to his list. But until he possesses that knowledge the study of bibliographies will only confuse his mind. Again, if he knows that a book exists and cannot remember the exact title or the date of it or some other detail, a bibliography is invaluable, provided always that it contains the book and that the student can find it. But if any one supposes that by working conscientiously through a bibliography he can easily select the right books to read, and the proper books on which to found his study of a new subject, he is in error. Bibliographies should be used not to provide a knowledge of books but to reveal to us our ignorance. So long as our ignorance of a subject exceeds our knowledge of it such aids are of little use.

How then, it may be asked, shall a student set about discovering books that he should study? It is not difficult to give a general answer to the question, though the student may find that the answer helps him but little. If he wants books, he must go where books are to be found, in short he must work in a library[1], and, if possible, in a library where the books are arranged in an intelligible order and where he can have access to the shelves. There by actual contact with books he must build up his own bibliography, and he must build it up round his subject and on the lines on which he means to treat it. It has already been pointed out that men may find the subjects which they wish to investigate in many ways, and of these two ways were described in particular. A man may either take a large and ill-defined subject and narrow

[1] I would add that so far as his opportunities allow, that library should be his own. It is only his own books that a student can use or misuse with absolute freedom.

it down, or take a small point and let it grow. In the first case he ought to have mastered the background of his subject in the process of selecting it, and his chief need will be the discovery of the special and obscurer books in which he may hope to find small details bearing upon the narrower field which he has finally chosen. His private bibliography may therefore be constructed for this purpose. If, on the other hand, he has begun with a small point, it is reasonable to suppose that in discovering it he has already become acquainted with some of the special literature, and that his chief need may be the discovery of the books which may enable him to enlarge his subject. In this case his private bibliography must be of another kind. But no rule can be laid down; the books that a student needs are fixed by the nature of his subject and his own intellectual resources. He alone can know these two conditions completely.

But in spite of this there are certain hints that may be useful. One of the best ways of finding the books needed is to hear of them from other students, especially from students more learned and more experienced in such matters than a beginner can be. To this end it is necessary to seek the acquaintance and company of men of learning and to offer to barter knowledge with them, giving book for book. Another way of work is to build round some book, choosing not necessarily the book of best repute or the latest book, but the book best known to the student. Certain qualities this book must possess; it must give references to the materials which the writer has used; it must deal with the other books on the subject, ignoring none worth study; it must permit the reader to discover its own weak points. Such a book may be made to serve as a starting point for the construction of the worker's own collection of printed authorities. But no one method will serve if the element of time has to be considered. A student working alone is sure to miss important books or obscure pamphlets at first; and the late discovery of such matter may involve the abandonment or reconstruction of much that he has done. It is true that this need not mean more than delay; but delay is disheartening and discouraging especially to the beginner, who because he is a beginner is sure to waste time and effort in other ways. Therefore let him use all methods that he can devise and all that he can learn from others in making his collection of printed authorities. Two matters only he must keep in his own hands.

In the first place he must see to it that his bibliography grows with his subject and along the lines of his subject. He must remember that he knows more about his subject than any one else, or at least intends to acquire that knowledge. He alone can anticipate the plan of his completed work, and see it finished before it is begun. The plan may change, details may be added or disappear, and the final form may differ completely from the first conception. But at every stage it is the writer and the writer alone who knows what the plan of the work is, and how it has grown and altered in the course of its execution. In consequence he is the only person who can settle finally the books to be consulted, applying to each the needful criticism and deciding the amount of study that each deserves. This amount will not be the same for all books; some, indeed, may require complete reading, some will contain sections that must be mastered, many will only contain a few passages to be noted. But the point is that the planning of the work and the selection of the books to be read must go on together, and be compelled to influence each other; this task the student cannot give up to any one else. He can get from any source and by any method the names of books to be consulted. Whether he will read them or not, and how much of them he will read, he must decide himself. In the same way he must also settle the number of books to be read. There are no spectres with more power to startle the strongest soul than the spectres of the dead books that lie on the shelves of all libraries. The stoutest student may well tremble before them; who can say in which of these may be hidden the clue to some puzzle? or, even more appalling thought, who

THE SEARCH FOR MATERIALS

can say that none of them contain an anticipation of that new discovery which is the chief distinction of the writer's work? There is, no doubt, one way in which these questions may be answered, namely, by reading them all. This heroic course should, however, be evaded, if possible, and, if evasion is impossible, should be openly rejected.

It is not wise to read too few books; it is simple folly to attempt to read too many. Yet there is one way of reading that may help the student to escape from this difficult choice, and it lies in the power of rapid and even superficial reading, sometimes called, by a metaphor taken from the dairy, 'skimming'. It is a powerful weapon and a valuable talent. It is so dangerous that it can only be commended with some hesitation, so indispensable that it must be acquired by those who do not possess it naturally. The danger lies in the fact that the reader who forms the habit of reading fast, of reading not by words or even sentences, but by whole pages or paragraphs sometimes loses the power of reading slowly and profoundly. He can grapple with a book, but cannot always master it. The best readers can use both methods and even know instinctively which to use at any time, when to turn over pages rapidly in search of the few passages they wish to discover for their own purpose, and when to slowly absorb into their own minds the whole book. They know also the value of the second or even the third reading, and the curious change in the estimate of a book which arises during such re-reading. Some students find it easiest to read a book first swiftly and eagerly, and base on that reading their statement of the problems to be stated and the likely solutions of them. With more knowledge they will then return to read it more carefully, and re-state the problems and solutions; and even discover new problems to solve, which they had not seen in their first attack. The reader who tries to 'tear the heart out of a book,' at his first encounter with it, knows how often he must return to his prey if he is to get all that is to be got from it. Nor can the most careful and profound student, who models his methods of absorption on those of the boa-constrictor, ever be sure that he will not find on a second or third persusal that there is still something that has evaded his comprehensive jaws.

No one will suppose that this brief discussion of printed material has left nothing unsaid. Yet it may be doubted whether it is possible to go much further into the matter without plunging into a depth of detail, in which the writer would soon find himself a mere flounderer. But it may be possible to mention a few points in which a book may be examined quickly. Everyone will have his own favourite method of testing or tasting a book, and the following method is only a specimen, not an infallible pre-

THE SEARCH FOR MATERIALS 83

scription. The first things to examine are the preface and introduction and the list of chapter headings. These parts of a book are often the last to be written, and may contain the author's own explanations of the contents of the book. They ought, at any rate, to give the reader some idea of what he is likely to find in it. The next point to notice is the style[1] in which the author writes and the way in which he arranges his matter. It is not necessary to read many pages in order to form an opinion on this point, and so to arrive at a rough estimate of the amount of work required to get at the information contained in the book. It is useless to condemn a book on a technical subject merely because it is hard to read and badly written. It may be necessary to dig out of it the information in spite of all the needless difficulties thrown in the way. The final test is to take a portion of the book about which the reader thinks he already knows something, and consider the authorities cited in the notes in support of the statements made in the text. The reader prefers that these citations should be sufficient to enable him to check the author's conclusions; authors sometimes prefer to exhibit their acquaintance with their authorities by heaping note on note and reference on reference, a method which

[1] Montaigne in his essay *Des livres* (Book II, ch. 10) says, speaking of History: " En ce gens d'estude des histories, il faut feuilleter, sans distinction toutes sortes d'aucteurs et vieils et nouveaux, et barragouins et françois, pour y apprendre des choses de quoy diversement ils traictent ".

has the advantage of discouraging any too great inquisitiveness on the part of the reader.

This examination of the authorities quoted will sometimes lead to curious discoveries. In the first forty-two pages of the second volume of Stubbs's *Constitutional History* the reader will find that in the notes there are a good many references to the Close Rolls for the early years of Henry the Third. At that point these references cease; nor is any reason given for the abandonment of this source of information. A hasty reader might well conclude either that there were no more Close Rolls in existence, or that the later rolls contained nothing worth quoting. The real explanation is simpler; at the date at which the author was writing the later rolls had never been printed, and Stubbs was unable to find the time needed to obtain material from the documents themselves. A hasty critic might be led to found upon this fact an indictment of the author and his book, and condemn both for shameless neglect of important sources. It may readily be admitted that Stubbs must have regretted that there were no more Close Rolls in print. Possibly in places his narrative may have suffered; but he had a great knowledge of his materials, an unrivalled power of using them, and an ingenious sagacity which enabled him to replace absent authorities by others. It would be difficult to discover any alteration in his narrative at the point in

THE SEARCH FOR MATERIALS 85

question, and the story continues with as much completeness and authority as if there were no change in his materials. An examination of his notes will show how he supplied the place of the unprinted Close Rolls, and show that where a modern student might have despaired, Stubbs was able to turn to other sources and continue his work unfalteringly.

This little story may serve as the bridge to carry us from printed to manuscript authorities. Fashion has decreed that no student to-day may base his research merely upon printed authorities. Perhaps, it may be suggested, too much stress is laid on this point. There may be some truth in Sainte-Beuve's protest, when he sums up a criticism of an edition of the letters of the Princesse des Ursins, in the following words.[1] Had one prepared oneself properly, he says, "on ne se piquera pas d'emblée d'être érudit avant d'avoir été tout uniment instruit (le grand et détestable travers du moment et le danger[2] littéraire de l'avenir) . . . on ne commencerait point par donner tête baissée dans l'inédit, avant d'avoir lu ce qui est imprimé

---

[1] *Causeries du Lundi*, vol. xiv, p. 266. The whole passage is worth reading.

[2] Information extracted from unpublished material carries with it curious charm, especially if it is acquired laboriously and from an obscure source. A man, who has turned over many thousands of sheets of parchment and finds after some months the name of William Shakespear, is not likely to be able to resist the temptation to value his discovery according to his toil. He has every right to rejoice; and yet there is a danger in magnifying the importance of new and unpublished material: it is so easy to think that all that comes from unknown sources is magnificent.

depuis deux siècles ". But Sainte-Beuve's protest is out of date, and rightly or wrongly any historical research not based partly on unpublished documents would be regarded with little approval to-day by any enthusiastic student.

Before such a student can begin his study of unprinted materials, he must know how to discover the materials he means to use, and his first step is to get some idea of where they are to be found. This task is not a difficult one; a very short enquiry will enable the beginner to discover where the materials he needs exist in quantity; he must, indeed, have made himself acquainted with that fact when he decided upon the subject of his book or article. His difficulties will only begin when he has exhausted the main masses of material. If he can he should stop there, and make no attempt to form a complete collection of unprinted and unused manuscripts. If he must go further, he will discover how hard it is to trace the wanderings of manuscripts; he will find himself following doubtful clues that may lead him into remote villages in England, or across continents to Pasadena on the shores of the Pacific. He may know the vexation of tracking down a manuscript and find, when he has clutched his prey, that it is only a copy of one he has already seen. His pleasures will be great, his successes may atone for his failures; and he will certainly see many collections of manuscripts and know the minds of those who keep and own them. The one thing he will not do is to complete his first piece of enquiry in any reasonable time. The beginner should find the main masses of his materials and content himself with these. The discovery of remote and scattered manuscripts he should leave until he has more time.

The [1] particular buildings, which may contain these main masses, he can find without much difficulty. As soon as he has found them, he will find himself in the presence of one or more of the keepers in charge of the manuscripts there deposited. It is a regrettable fact that there are not enough archangels in residence on the earth, since many problems could be simplified by putting a seraph in charge of all the search-rooms frequented by the devotees of historical research. As things are, there occasionally arises a certain sense of strain between the custodian and the researcher. Their duties and interests are to some extent conflicting; and in moments of invective either may forget this important fact. The student who rightly wishes to know how he can readily discover the documents he needs, may easily be led to ask for information as to the contents of the documents, which he means to examine, and to expect some guidance and even assistance on this point. He will feel and even express

---

[1] I write this section as one *destrictus ensis cui super impia cervice pendet.*

surprise when a custodian replies without any sense of shame that he is not in a position to give such information and knows nothing about the documents in question. On the other hand he may be equally startled by receiving a willing and complete answer to his inquiries; and he may often be tempted to extremities of praise and blame, neither of which are deserved. By degrees he will begin to understand the habit of mind of those whom he consults, and the way in which they work.

The duty of the keepers of documents is to provide for their safe custody, to preserve the history of the various collections in their charge, to assign all stray documents to their proper classes, to form new classes where and only where new classes are needed, and to provide proper means of reference. For these purposes they must know the contents of some of the material in their charge and have a general knowledge of the whole of the collection or at any rate of a large part of it. It follows that a student cannot expect much more than that he should be given full information as to the general principles on which the collection is arranged, and as to the means of reference that exist; and if this information is not available either orally or in writing, he has proper cause for feeling some annoyance[1]. He will have to play a double part, find

---

[1] There are, of course, many cases in which the student will find no general arrangement, no classes and no lists. The beginner will be well advised if he avoids those collections. At one time it was, for example,

THE SEARCH FOR MATERIALS

out for himself what the documents are, and what is in them. But in many of the most important cases, he will find that this is done for him; and he may then expect a good deal of help in discovering the classes of documents he needs, though he must always remember that his intention is to know more than anyone else does about his chosen subject, and that in consequence he will have to select for himself his own material and devise his own methods of using it. Nevertheless he may get much more; there are uncovenanted as well as covenanted mercies. There are but few keepers of manuscripts who have not deviated from the strict line of their duties. Even the sternest archivist who from a sense of duty has renounced " historical work on his own account "[1] will have been obliged to study minutely some part of the documents in his care, and may even have published some of his researches, excusing himself by calling his sin " an exercise to keep alive his interest in history ". There are few men possessed of knowledge who do not enjoy imparting it. The student can usually discover these hidden possessors of knowledge; a little diplomatic violence may be needed to overcome the first barriers, but when this has been done, the enquirer

---

not easy to work either at Pampeluna or at Naples. Something may have been done in both cases since those days. Preliminary enquiry should always be made on such points. But the condition of a Record Office may alter quickly.

[1] *The Care of Documents,* by C. Johnson, p. 42 (Helps for the Students of History).

may get the extra help he requires, and often win not only that help but an intellectual friendship that will be offered to him as fully as he desires to accept it.

Any student who wishes to make use of a collection of manuscripts must begin by considering the nature of the collection. He will find that there are two principal classes, and as generally happens a large number of intermediate examples which fall between the two well marked types. These two well marked types may be described as the archive-type or record office and the museum or library type. The distinction between them rests on the fact that in the archive-type 'the collection of documents has been made for the purpose of preserving records which were made for purposes of administration or in the proceedings of law-courts; so that in every case, unless some accident or error has intervened, it should be possible to discover at once the origin of every document, the place from which it was brought into its present place of deposit and to ascertain on enquiry the purpose for which it was made. Every document in a record office has had a definite place in some administrative or legal process, and unless unwise methods have obscured that fact there should be little difficulty in discovering the origin and purpose of any part of the collection. On the other hand in the case of collections of manuscripts preserved in a library or museum the collection has been formed accidentally. The documents are of various kinds and come from many sources, and often there is no means by which their history can be readily discovered, if indeed it can be discovered at all. They have been acquired at different times, sometimes singly, sometimes in small parcels, sometimes in large blocks; and their arrangement in the museum is necessarily and properly dependent on the order in which they have come into the hands of their keepers. The large blocks may represent a private or in some cases a public group of documents originally formed and still preserved as a collection of an archive type. They may be the whole or a large part of the papers of a family or of an official, and thus have a definite unity and a logical relation between themselves. On the other hand they may be the accumulation of some collector of manuscripts, who has bought widely on no particular principle, or obtained in other ways documents in which he was interested from all sorts of places. It follows that in dealing with collections of the archive-type the researcher may expect to find that the classification of the document should help him to understand the documents themselves, while in collections of the museum-type he must regard himself as fortunate when this happens to be the case. The methods of study will in consequence differ to some extent. It will be easiest to begin with a discussion of collections of the archive-type, easiest not only for the reader but also for the writer; and it will also be easiest to select as a particular case the collection of documents preserved in the Public Record Office[1] in London. Any one, who for the first time enters that building, may well think that it will be an impossible task to discover and examine all the documents necessary for the study of even the smallest subject within the lifetime of any man. This mood of despair will not last for long; possibly it may be followed by a reaction and the student may begin to cherish a hope that the task is really not an impossible one; finally he may be able to arrive at a correct estimate of the work needed for his subject, an estimate which may induce him to a further limitation of its scope. In order to acquire this knowledge he will have to learn something at any rate of the collection as a whole and the system of classification used in the arrangement of the various documents. There are many books which will assist him to obtain this information, and many ways in which he can find out their names and qualities, and no account of them will be attempted here. All that can be done is to give the reader certain warnings and hints which may save him some

---

[1] The practice of the Public Record Office is not necessarily based on that of other record offices; still less is it a model followed by them. Every collection of archives has its own peculiar problems and its own solutions of them. But the general types of work and the general problems are the same in all, whether in the Archives Nationales at Paris, or in the Archivio of the Vatican at Rome, or in the Castle of Simancas. To deal fully with more than one such collection would stretch this chapter beyond pardon.

THE SEARCH FOR MATERIALS

trouble. It has been said above that every document in a record office has had a definite place in some administrative or legal process, and that it should therefore be possible to discover at once the origin of any document and to investigate the purpose for which it was made. It was also suggested that the classification of the documents would assist the student in such enquiries. This is not always true, and it is the first business of the enquirer to ascertain how far he may trust the classification of those documents which he decides to use. In most cases he will find that the classification is definitely based upon the origin and purpose of the documents themselves. In certain classes he will discover evidence of confusion, confusion not necessarily introduced in modern times but often of long standing and now impossible to correct. No one, for instance, can doubt that most of the rolls now called 'Carte Antique' and treated as Chancery documents, were really drawn up by Exchequer scribes; but the misdescription is at least as early as the fourteenth century and the origin of the blunder can only be guessed. Again, he may come upon classes formed on mistaken principles. Documents have been placed together sometimes because they were alike in form or purpose, sometimes because they are related to the same geographical area, and sometimes because a collection has been made to enable some historian to have in one mass all the documents which he needed[1]. More rarely classes may be found which seem to represent mere residues left over from the sortation of documents whose nature and origin were unknown to their custodians. It must not be thought that these pit-falls await the student wherever he may turn, or that he will be left in ignorance of their existence, but they are a danger against which he should be on his guard. A little experience will make it easy for him to perceive the traps before he falls into them.

It has been said that the enquirer should begin by finding out something about the collection as a whole. It should be added that he should make no attempt at obtaining more than a superficial knowledge. He knows enough as soon as he can select the classes of documents which he must examine. In making his choice of the area in which he has determined to look for his subject he will have attained part of the knowledge needed for this selection, and have decided at any rate upon some limits in time, which will allow him to exclude many classes of documents as irrelevant to his purpose. The further study of that area necessary for the discovery and definition of his subject will enable him to revise the results of the first examination; some classes, at first included in his survey, will have been excluded, others at first excluded will have

---

[1] The accidental character of many of these classes is clearly marked by the official description of them as *Special Collections*.

THE SEARCH FOR MATERIALS 95

been found to require examination. The key to problems of selection will have been discovered, and the student will see that the selection of the documents to be examined depends on the connexion between his subject and the existing classification of the materials. If that connexion is close and complete, his task will be the lighter; if it is loose or absent, it will be harder. If, for instance, the subject chosen is the administration of a definite office during a definite period, the records of that office[1] during that period will constitute the main mass of materials to be examined. The first step, therefore, is to ascertain whether the records for that period exist as a class; if this is the case, the enquiry in its first stages can be confined to that class, and its results will show whether for full and complete knowledge the enquiry must be extended to other classes and to a wider period. In many cases no such connexion will be found; the records, for instance, of the King's Council for the earlier period do not exist as a whole, but are scattered among many classes. Again no one interested in the details of financial administration can hope to confine his researches within accurate limits of time; he will certainly have to examine records both before and

[1] It should be noted that an office may be abolished, and its archives transferred to its successor. The result is likely to be some confusion. The records of the Board of Trade and Plantations passed to the Colonial Office in this way; and the records of the Exchequer of Receipt have wandered from one office to another in a complicated fashion. It may happen, of course, that the abolished office has no successor, and that its archives become masterless.

after his chosen period, if his research is to be complete and intelligent. Nor in dealing with this subject can he even confine himself to the records of the main financial department, the Exchequer. These subjects, it will be seen, are of one kind; they deal with problems of administration. They belong to the class of subjects where the relation between the subject and the class of material is the closest. Subjects of this kind are indeed the only subjects where the relation is in a way inevitable unless it has been destroyed, since it exists for the simple reason that the records were themselves prepared for purposes of administration, those purposes being the very things which the researcher desires to study. Even in the case of legal subjects, where an equally close connexion between subject and record-material might be expected, more difficulty will often be encountered in relating the subject to the nature of the records. Any one who endeavours to trace to its end a single law-suit through voluminous plea-rolls, will soon discover that plea-rolls are primarily meant to record pleadings and procedure rather than legal principles and that for these he must go to the Year Books or Reports, and to treatises on law; when he has done this he will still need the plea-rolls to understand what he has found in these sources. If his subject is concerned neither with legal nor with administrative history, he cannot expect to find for all periods natural classes of records formed to suit his purposes. If he is writing political history, he will find no such classes until the Secretary of State, or at any rate his ancestor the Secretary, has risen to his full importance and the State Paper Office has been instituted to keep the State Papers which the Secretary receives and issues or uses for his own purposes. In the same way every new office which achieves a status of its own will acquire a special archive, and the date of the creation of each new office will fix the date at which the student can expect to find natural and independent classes ready to his hand. It is indeed possible that he may find artificial classes formed for special purposes among the records of any period, but such classes are seldom to be trusted implicitly. They usually contain documents that should not have been placed there and always omit documents that should have been included. They must always be used with great care, and some suspicion.

The subjects so far discussed all have some connexion at some periods with the classification of documents; there are however other classes of subjects where no such connexion can be expected. The facts of economic or social history may be found in many places; and even to-day the writer on such subjects cannot expect to find all his materials in the archives of the Board of Trade or the Ministry of Labour or the Ministry of Health. In some cases, indeed, the student may even find that there is nothing in the Public Record Office of primary importance to him, and that all he can hope to find in that collection are a few accidental facts which he may use to illustrate his writings. Specimens of wall-paper exist in the Public Record Office, and there are leather bags to be seen there; but the student interested in the history of those arts will scarcely be tempted to make researches there, until he has exhausted more promising places.

Enough has now been said in explanation of the rule laid down above that on the subject chosen by the student depends the selection of the class or classes of documents on which he will work. It is time to come to the means that exist for discovering first the nature of the classes, and next that of the individual documents composing them. The main authority for the study of the classes is the official guide[1] to the whole collection; and it must be said that it is not and cannot be an easy book for the beginner to use. At first he will probably expect too much from it. He will forget that it is not intended to deal with the arrangement of records from the point of view of the writers of monographs, still less from the point of view of the writer of a particular monograph, but that it

---

[1] *A Guide to the Public Manuscripts preserved in the Public Record Offices*, by M. S. Giuseppi, F.S.A., 2 vols., 1923. This is the latest form of guide. For the history of the classification the earlier guides are still useful.

THE SEARCH FOR MATERIALS

describes the whole collection from an impartial stand-point, leaving to each user the task of adapting its information to his own purposes. He will, it is true, find in it short accounts of the origin and nature of the various classes, and short sketches of the documents contained in them; and though this information is not and cannot be complete or satisfactory it will give the enquirer something on which he may build. A little reflexion will show him that if such a book were able to anticipate every purpose for which a document can be used, it could only have been written by persons acquainted with all history whose existence would render his own superfluous. A little more experience will enable him to see that in this book he possesses a means of discovering at any rate the class of documents most needed for his research. In his study of that class he will soon find other classes to which he must turn to complete his enquiry. In fact his main difficulty will lie in knowing where to stop.

Probably the chief value of the book to the beginner will be found to consist in the information which it will give him as to the means of reference to the documents contained in the classes. These consist of Lists, Indexes, Descriptive Lists[1], Calendars, and complete Transcripts of Documents; and all of these may

---

[1] A type-written List of Lists and Indexes is kept in the Record Office; there are copies in some libraries.

be either in print or in manuscript. The nature of the lists and descriptive lists will be clear after a very slight acquaintance. A simple list deals with a class of documents which are all of the same kind, and which by reason of their size can be dealt with only by a common description applicable to all of them. All that is necessary is a date and a reference for each document in the class. Any detailed description of each document in these cases is either needless or impossible. No mere list can possibly contain any account of the contents of a Pipe Roll; any attempt to insert such an account into a list would be a failure, and only produce a volume unwieldly in size and useless in its information. A descriptive list is intended to deal with documents of a small size, where a simple list would be insufficient. Such documents are often undated and some description of each is needed to enable custodians and researchers to identify the documents in the list. In some cases it may also be possible to get a rough idea of the contents of the document from the description in the list, but this is not always the case; the possibility of using a descriptive list in this way depends on the nature of the documents listed. All these points will become clear after a very brief acquaintance with these lists. Nor need we spend much time on the consideration of complete transcripts. They are intended to contain every word that is in the original and may be used instead of the original, subject to the possibility of error in the transcription. But the nature and use of calendars is a more complicated matter. An entry in a calendar is rarely a complete transcript of the original; it is far more often an abstract of a translation of that entry. It is intended to give the facts contained in that entry, names of places and persons, and to show the formal relations between them created by the document or expressed in it. Now the documents treated in this way may be of the most varied kinds; they may be notes or memoranda, familiar letters, formal letters, administrative orders, writs, royal grants, private deeds, legal proceedings, inquisitions and so forth. No one system of abstracting can be devised applicable to all of these classes; and no rules can be laid down that will really cover all the varieties of treatment that may be needed to deal properly even with documents that might seem capable of uniform treatment. In consequence the user of a calendar must always remember that within wide limits the method pursued in the making of it depends on the private judgement of the man who made it.

Nevertheless there are some points worth making, and as these points bear not only upon the use of calendars but also on the general theory of documents, they must be made in a separate section and introduced by a discussion of some general principles. Every document, excluding mere notes and memoranda, consists of a framework and a set of names and special facts, special that is to the single document considered. The framework may be used for composition of any document of the same kind, and is the formal part of the document. It may be spoken of as the form. The names and facts may be termed the material[1] of the document. Any one who has ever seen a modern lease will at once know what is meant. The form of the lease is the printed part, and with a few exceptions is the same for all leases or at any rate for a large class of leases; the material of the lease consists of the names of the parties, the description of the premises, the amount of the rent and any special clauses added in particular cases. The form is the constant part, made according to a fixed pattern contained in precedent books or treatises on the art of conveying property or interests in property; the material varies from lease to lease. This case has been chosen as one that is familiar to most readers and because it is easy to understand. It also emphasizes the fact that it is in legal documents that the distinction between form and material is most obvious and important. The same principle exists, however, in nearly all types, no less in letters than in deeds, and sometimes in ways not easy to detect. In letters for instance it may be very

---

[1] 'Form' and 'matter' are, of course, logical terms. The reader must be warned that there is no security that the connexion between this passage and traditional logic is more than accidental.

difficult to be quite sure which parts of the letter are form and which material. The beginning of a letter, except in the case of familiar and intimate letters, is formal and so is the part which precedes the signature; and the forms are often carefully selected. A student of history writing to a Marquis, who is also a Bishop, to request permission to work among the papers of the family will have to make a careful study of the proper form to use if he is to attain his purpose, and will find that a good deal of the letter will consist of form and the material will be small. On the other hand a letter written to the same nobleman by his wife will be nearly all material and contain very little form. In both cases the address on the envelope will be in strict form.

It has been said that the form of a document is the constant part of it; and this is nearly true of documents written at one period of time. But form like everything else has its own history and changes from period to period, and the discovery and explanation of these changes is, like poker, 'a fascinating and highly oncertain game'. The methods and rules of the game constitute what is called 'Diplomatic', and may be applied to the study of single documents and to classes of documents. In this book these methods can only be illustrated very briefly and the illustrations will be chosen to display the strength and weakness of the methods used. Let us begin with an imaginary case.

Suppose that it was necessary to discover the names of the adherents of some great man living in the earlier part of the fifteenth century, and that for this purpose the enquirer were to examine all the chancery proceedings in which that great man was a petitioner. Now every person putting forward a bill in chancery had to provide pledges for certain reasons which do not concern us here. The names of those pledges are entered on the bill at the foot. It is not impossible that there might be several such bills, and that there would be some connexion between the petitioner and the pledges. It would be a useful thing to note down the names of the pledges. Let us suppose that the names were John Egyll and Henry Lyoun, and that these two gentlemen went down in the student's notes as adherents of the great man. Now it might happen that the student would stop there content. But it might also happen that he would look further, and if he did he might come upon a bill in which the names of the pledges were William Pepper and John Mustard or Henry Beefe and William Mutton, and if he went on still further he would find that the pledges named in all bills in Chancery were called John Doe and Richard Roe. By this time he would have begun to doubt whether the bird and the beast in the first bill were real people or whether they were simply part of the form of the bill. If he went any further with the enquiry, he would finally conclude that there was a date before which the pledges were real people, and another date after which they were mere ghosts; and that for the intervening period there was no saying which they were. Finally he might express his conclusion in general terms. Names, he might say, are not always part of the material of a document, they may be part of the form[1]; and he might add that changes in the form of a document may occur gradually and that there may always be a debatable period during which the transitional forms will exist, and uncertainty must be expected. Further experiments in 'Diplomatic' may lead him to introduce a proviso and add that where a definite cause can be shown to exist for a change of form, the debatable period will not exist. Even this will not end the matter; it will still be necessary to remember that the man who drafted the document may have been ignorant of the existence of the cause or even refused to alter the form in compliance with the new rule. A few more instances must suffice to make the meaning of 'Diplomatic' methods clear. M. Delisle succeeded in establishing that after Henry II had done penance for the death of Beckett, the royal style was changed from 'Henricus rex Anglorum, etc.' to 'Henricus dei gratia rex Anglorum, etc.', and thus provided a criterion by which the undated charters of

[1] In some extreme cases apparent matters of fact will be found to be merely form. Statements in 'Proofs of Age' are no evidence of the reality of the facts declared to have happened.

that king could be assigned to one of two periods. But the general question of the study of 'Diplomatic' lies outside the purpose of this book, and has only been introduced here in order to explain the nature of calendars and their limitations. It has been said that nearly all entries in them are abstracts of the original entries. They are abstracts, and that means that part of the original must be omitted; in fact as much as possible must be omitted. Now the first thing to go will be the formal part; it will be replaced by a brief statement of its effect and of the relations created by it expressed in words that are not necessarily even a translation of any part of the original. Many phrases and clauses will wholly disappear. A worker who knows the forms used in the documents calendared may be able to guess what lies behind the abstract, but even he can only conjecture. It follows necessarily that for the study of form all calendars are useless to the student; for this purpose he must go to the original. With the material the user of a calendar is on firmer ground; the entries in a calendar ought in most cases to preserve the whole of the material existing in the original, and in most cases they will do this. But there are exceptions. Where the originals to be calendared consist of letters and other documents, which are only formal to a small extent, if at all, a full abstract will be hardly shorter than the original, and the maker of the calendar will be left to find his way between two alternatives, neither of which is satisfactory. He must either aim at brevity and sacrifice some of the material, or he must make the retention of the whole of his material his main object and so produce abstracts in name which in fact will be little less than transcripts. He may try to follow a middle course, and make the length of his abstract depend on his estimate of the importance or novelty of the information contained in the original or on the legibility of the document. In this case he runs a risk; his estimate cannot be the same as that of every user of the calendar, and he will have to meet the criticisms of those who accuse him of needless length and of those who will find that his omissions have made his work useless to them. He will be wise to pray for a broad back and a thick skin. Let us leave him to his prayers, and return to the student who is using his results.

For him there is only one effective way of criticism. The first step is to find out the scheme of the calendar, read the introduction to the first volume, note carefully the original source or sources used, and ascertain whether it is a complete calendar or a selection of entries, and examine the principles on which the selections or omissions have been made. When this has been done, an hour or two should be spent in comparing the abstracts with the originals and in studying the plan pursued by the maker of the calendar and so getting to know where the calendar will be useful for the purpose in hand, and where it will fail. Other methods of criticism depend on the nature of the documents calendared and those methods the student must devise for himself according to his needs.

If we now turn to collections of the museum-type; we shall find that most of the principles here stated will apply, provided that we remember that the classes are generally not founded upon the origin and purpose of the documents contained in them. This fact increases the difficulty of the task before the student. He is bound to rely almost entirely on the means of reference provided for him, and only in that way can he discover the documents he needs for his purpose. These means of reference differ according to the practice of the library or museum and the classification there used; and it may be as well to warn the student that the technical terms used in them may differ widely from those used in record offices. Thus the term 'charter' in the lists of the British Museum is used in a far more general sense than in the lists of the Public Record Office. The first step for the student is to get hold of the terminology and the meaning of the various classes and their history.[1] His next step will be to examine the means of reference

[1] For the British Museum he will find much of what he wants in *A Student's Guide to the Manuscripts of the British Museum*, by Julius P. Gilson (Helps for Students of History, S.P.C.K.).

THE SEARCH FOR MATERIALS

which exist for the various classes. Finally he must face the question of the selection of the best class to examine. It will be agreed that this is not an easy task. In all probability he will have to take all the help he can obtain; he will have to take counsel with his fellow-students, with older and wiser authorities, and endeavour to obtain the advantage of those 'uncovenanted mercies' already mentioned. In the British Museum there are also 'covenanted mercies'. There is always the class-catalogue. This has been formed by taking from the special catalogues of each class the descriptions of the documents in these classes, and sorting all the slips so made under subject headings. It need hardly be said that this catalogue gives much help to the beginner. From it he can find at once the references to many documents that he must examine, even if a mere glance reveals their uselessness. Its limitations are as obvious as they are inevitable. The subject headings represent the opinions of the men who settled them; they are intended to help every kind of research and cannot be perfectly adapted to the requirements of any one student. It might be supposed that more could have been done by the use of cross-references; but a little consideration will convince the critic that any advantage that he could acquire in this way would have been annihilated, since the class-catalogue would probably never have been finished at all. Sooner or later he will have to supplement the references he has obtained from the class-catalogue by adding to them others derived from the special catalogues[1] of those classes which he has found to be of most importance for his purpose. This is not so hopeless a task as it might seem; he will often find that in the various classes the documents he needs lie in groups. This will happen because the man who made the original collection will have taken his documents from a limited number of sources and have kept together those which have a common origin and a common character and date. Moreover, to a student of history those documents will naturally be most important which have escaped from record offices or which by some accident have remained in the hands of official persons who have never surrendered them to their proper custodians. It is to these classes that the historical student will first turn. Their names and their history he must discover for himself. Any details that could be given here would be brief and misleading and only an imperfect repetition of what has been done elsewhere in a fuller and better way by those who have more knowledge.

The Public Record Office and the British Museum have been chosen here as types, because they are the collections in which most English-speaking students of

---

[1] These special catalogues often omit separate items, and group many manuscripts under one descriptive heading. The catalogue of the Harleian manuscripts is an instance of this method of working.

history will naturally look for the materials they require. It is hardly necessary to say that there are even in England many other places in which students may wish to work. Nor need it be said that every record office and every library or museum will have its own methods of classification and its own system of indexes and means of reference. It may even be suspected that in some cases these aids to the student will be absent or at least imperfect, and that now and then the custodians will be more eager to exclude than to admit the enquirer. This will not happen by reason of any perversity in their hearts, but simply because in many cases records are in the keeping of men who have other duties and no time or money to spend upon the care of the records in their charge. Again, the methods of classification and the nature of the means of reference vary from country to country. The student can find in various books enough information on these points to be able to anticipate the difficulties he will meet with and the assistance he can hope to obtain in particular cases. Here no attempt can be made to give such information. But he may be assured that in all cases he must start by getting a superficial knowledge of the collection as a whole and of its classification. Thence he should proceed to ascertain the main classes which he must examine, and then select the documents which his subject compels him to study. Any help that he can get he will need for these preliminary steps; all final decisions must remain in his own hands.

With a few principles of criticism this section must be brought to an end. In the use of books no trained reader ever forgets that the basis of all criticism is the character of the writer and the nature of his materials; but even experienced workers are apt to forget to apply this rule to manuscripts and above all to records. These seem to carry with them a charm which dulls criticism. The student forgets the man who wrote them and regards them as ultimate authorities behind which he ought not to try to pass. Now it is of course true that in the case of most records we can hardly expect to know even the name of the scribe, and that of his character we are likely to remain in complete ignorance. It may even be admitted that in many cases we can only guess at the materials he had before him. These facts, however, are only a reason for using greater caution and not for abandoning all attempt at criticism. It has often been pointed out that 'records were drawn up for temporary purposes and not for the instruction of posterity' and it may be added that the man who wrote them had no reason for explaining what those purposes were, and still less reason for explaining his own opinions and ideas. The purpose of a document was known to those who used it without explanation; the character and political ideas of the scribe were his own business, and im-

THE SEARCH FOR MATERIALS

pertinent in a official document. Yet these things are of the utmost importance in interpreting a record. A trivial instance will show into what error students may fall by only looking at the face of a document. All numbers in medieval records are written in roman numerals; writers may be found who will marvel at the skill which enabled medieval computers to work sums in this cumbrous notation. They forget that a man who writes down his results in roman figures has not necessarily used them in his calculations, and they are apparently too little curious of the history of arithmetic to attempt to discover what methods were actually employed. This is a small matter; more serious are the errors produced by attributing to medieval scribes social and political ideas which had hardly come into existence at the date when they were writing their daily task of official work. Statesmen and officials to-day are not considered to possess minds enriched by the knowledge of advanced political thought; and though we cannot be sure that this was true of the statesmen and officials of the fifteenth century, for instance, it is hazardous to attribute to them a prophetic knowledge of the principles of later ages. Even ethical conceptions change; though they change more slowly than most of us would wish to believe; and it is very easy to forget this process of change, and to attribute to the men of one century moral principles which they would have repudiated. It is all the more easy to fall into this error, because ethical conceptions are continually confused by the normal human reluctance to make practical life obey accepted moral doctrine. Perhaps the history of the doctrine of the right of individual citizens to hold, express and advocate private opinions shows the difficulty as well as any other instance. Three[1] stages seem discoverable in the story of this complicated subject. Up to the date of the Reformation it was generally held that no such right existed, at any rate in religious questions, the only questions commonly discussed in those times. With the Reformation began a period in which any advocate of a doctrine claimed the right for himself and in practice denied it to his opponents. By degrees there grew up a theory of mutual toleration, coupled with a denial that such a right could be claimed for opinions held to be destructive of society or morally pernicious, or under special circumstances opposed to the policy of the government. The line thus drawn between opinions that may be expressed and those that may rightly be forbidden, is a shifting one; and the methods of repression vary in every form of society. Questions which provoke repression either from governments or from unauthorized organizations of private citizens are still very numerous. It seems

[1] This sketch necessarily omits many details; it is only intended to show the difficulty that attends on the discussion of all ethical subjects.

THE SEARCH FOR MATERIALS

that the general view taken to-day is that the free expression of opinion is the right of every individual, provided that he uses it rightly. The historian who applies this rather vague criterion to the past, will assuredly be in danger of misinterpreting the motives of the men who lived in other days.

It may be hard, even impossible, to take all these factors into account. Yet if we wish to avoid error, we must remember that such factors exist and that we must not substitute for our ignorance of the character of the scribe our own frame of mind with our own mental, political and ethical ideas. Nor must we push our methods of interpretation so strictly as to extract from a document information which it is not capable of giving, though we may and indeed must use all our ingenuity to discover all that can be found in it. A natural desire to know will urge us to do this; and that desire can only be kept from leading us into error by critical methods. The consideration of the scribe[1] and his materials will be the best foundation on which these can be built.

The reader may here ask, are there not other sources of error and other remedies to be applied. Assuredly there are; he will find them described in the *De Augmentis Scientiarum* of Francis Bacon and

[1] The best method of considering the scribe and his materials is to imagine him at work. An admirable opportunity for the use of this method is to be found in the study of *Cahiers de Doléances* entrusted to the members of the States General of 1789 by their constituents. For a brief account see *Cambridge Modern History*, vol. viii, p. 134.

in his *Novum Organum* under the name of 'Idola'.[1] But here I can only answer his enquiry in the words of Richard son of Neal, Bishop of London, the author of the *Dialogus de Scaccario*:

"Magnum est quod quaeris et alterius egens inquisitionis. . . . Vereor quidem ne si pluribus onerato novam sarcinam imponerem sub pondere deficeres."

Let us turn to other matters. The methods of error are many, and no book can contain them all.

---

[1] Are there not also Ernst Bernheim's *Lebrbuch des historischer Methode* and the *Introduction aux études historiques,* by Charles V. Langlois and Ch. Seignobos? Every historical student should know the backs of these books at any rate. Bacon has the merit of brevity.

IV

NOTES AND THE MAKING OF THEM

IF the enquirer were fortunate enough to possess a mind retentive of all information required by him, this chapter would be needless and the taking of notes would be unknown. All that any such writer could need would be ready in his memory and like the chorus in "The Tragedy of Eriphyle," he might proudly declare that all his sources might be summed up in the one line "Its native ingenuity sufficed my self-taught diaphragm"[1]. But for man, as he is, notes are an unfortunate necessity, and no part of a researcher's task is harder than the making of them. For a note may be of any size and of any complexion. It may be a mere reference followed by a couple of words indicating the information to be discovered if the reference is used; it may be a complete and

---

[1] From "Fragment of a Greek Tragedy" in *The Bromsgrovian* (8th June, 1883), New Series, vol. ii, no. 5: signed A.E.H. I am told that there is another version published elsewhere, but have not been able to find it.

lengthy transcript of a passage from a book or document; it may be a critical estimate of the value of an authority. It may be meant for use in the research that is being pursued; it may be meant to be put aside for future reference, or even be made from unselfish motives for the use of another worker; and finally notes may be made for none of these purposes but merely for the gratification of the curious passion of note-making which possesses some minds. Even if this last class be omitted from our survey as a perverse taste, it is not easy to find any one formula or system in which to include all the others. All that can be said in general is that the notes to be taken and the way in which they are taken both depend on the use to which they are to be put. Unless this rule, that notes are meant for use and are taken for a purpose, is kept in mind, mischief will certainly befall the researcher; mischief of two kinds; his notes will be either too many or too few, and will contain the information that he does not want and not the information that he needs.

Now as has been said all notes are a substitute for knowledge; a collection of notes is an extension of our memories. Just as Themistocles desired to possess the art of forgetting, so every researcher should aim at knowing when not to take notes. The first point to consider is the accessibility of materials, and the first rule seems to be that the length and detail of a note depends on the difficulty of finding the material required. The accessibility of a book lying on the student's writing table is very high, though not as high as the accessibility of a book lying open at the passage needed for immediate use. A book in the next room is less accessible; and a book in the Vatican library, of which no other copy exists, may be accessible only at a great cost. But it is not only questions of distance that have to be considered in estimating the accessibility of material. It is also needful to take account of the fact that the alertness of the researcher and his power of insight vary from day to day. The passage in the book lying open on the table, which to-day seems to throw a new and startling light on some problem, three weeks ago may have seemed of little moment, three weeks hence may seem a bare statement of fact, a thing known to all men.[1] The fact remains accessible, the application of it is lost. And so by the use of these and other criteria of the same kind we may arrive at a rough measure of the necessity of making a note and of the amount and kind of detail with which a note should be made.

[1] Cf. Niebuhr, *History of Rome*, vol. i, p. 356 [Translation by Hare and Thirlwall (1847), 4th edition]. "In a mass of utter confusion, a single spot, which others have overlooked, will often strike an observing eye, but no distinct consciousness of it is retained, because it is only an insulated fragment. It recurs to the memory, when anything else connected with it is met with, but it is often only a transient light which falls upon the darkness; and even he on whom it has shone forgets what it revealed to him."

It has already been said that there are three rational motives for making notes, the intention to use them for the research then in hand and two others which need not be dealt with at this point. Now at the back of any successful research there must lie a clear conception of the purpose of the research, and a definite knowledge of the subject. It is often suggested that all that is required on this point is to select a subject and that the student may then proceed in all confidence to collect his materials, make his notes and finally expand his notes into the form of a treatise. Those who work in this way will produce a result of a kind, but it will be exactly the kind of result which induces in the reader respect for the energy of the author and compassion for himself. All the necessary facts may be there; evidence of careful and conscientious work may abound; but one thing will be lacking, the skeleton of thought needed to make the book an intelligible whole. It will be lacking because the writer, absorbed in perfecting the mechanism of his process, has never practised the art of thinking. He has accumulated facts without a plan, and has hoped that in the process a plan would emerge of itself, and in the end the accumulation of facts has mastered him, not he them. The remedy is not difficult to find, and it may conveniently be expressed in the form of a paradox. Write your treatise first, and make your notes afterwards.

This maxim, being expressed in the form of a paradox, does not mean what it appears to say. It is, indeed, the object of a paradox to state truth in the guise of an absurdity, in order that the reader may first experience the pleasure of revolt and then swing back to a reluctant admission that it is not really as absurd as it sounds. There can, indeed, be no doubt that the life of a student would be pleasant, if he could literally obey the precept. It would be delightful to sit down with pen and paper and write out of one's head some sixty thousand words, marking here and there the places where references should be inserted to notes to be added at the foot of each page and leaving blank spaces in the text to be filled in with the appropriate extracts. This done, it would be amusing to collect the notes and extracts needed and insert them into their proper places, and finally sign one's name at the end with a conscious delight in a duty successfully accomplished, and so begin to enjoy a well earned leisure. The paradox seems to suggest that such a course is possible; it is only the experience of actual work that insists on our setting it aside as impracticable, a mere ideal not to be realized in the sublunary sphere. But though we discard the plain words of the paradox, it may be possible to find a reasonable meaning behind them. At any rate it is worth trying. Impossible as it may be to write a finished treatise without notes, it may be possible to do something, something in the way of a project or at any rate a sketch. The mere fact that a subject has been chosen involves the possession of some sort of knowledge, some amount of material, existing not necessarily or even preferably in the form of notes, but certainly in matter stored in the mind. Some students may prefer to keep it there in a flexible, half-expressed form, trusting to their memory and readiness to find words for it as they are needed. They have the main lines of their work continually present with them, they know where the notes they need will fit in to the mental scheme; they can modify the scheme as fresh discoveries may require; they have their treatise unwritten in their heads, and make their notes to those unwritten pages. This is a good way, it is perhaps the best way, but it has one serious defect. It is a way that puts a heavy strain on the worker, on his memory and his mental power. A short piece of work of about five or six thousand words in length on a sharply defined subject can be carried out in this way by a skilled researcher, who can keep the outlines of his work clearly in his head. A worker with still greater experience and greater power may be able to break up a larger work into small parts and by taking each part separately may succeeed at a price in dispensing with any plan but the one he carries in his mind. But even he will pay a price, and the beginner cannot always afford to subject himself to the necessary strain. If he thinks he can, he may run the risk, and he may succeed. The one thing he should not do is to start to make notes without having a plan of his work somewhere.

If these arguments should suffice to convince him of the wisdom of such a method, the next step is to determine the form and content of such a plan. In the process of finding and selecting his subject, he must necessarily have learnt something about it, enough at any rate to be able to describe it. Some part of that description he may even have committed to writing. His obvious course is to begin by writing down all he knows, all he surmises, and all he wants to know. It will not be wasted labour; as he writes the form and arrangement of the complete work will be determined; he will discover what he knows and, what is still more important, what he does not know. Here and there he may even be able to add to his knowledge. It will all be tentative and experimental, and detail is needless; neither should it be long, nor need much time be given to it. Vagueness of expression and slip-shod writing should be avoided, and no pains should be spared which may be needed to produce a clear and intelligible statement. But the form and content must be chosen by the worker himself according to his taste. Some will prefer a list of headings grouped under larger headings, showing the several sections and the chapters in which they are to come; others may prefer a connected narrative form; others may find a chronological statement more to their liking; and in some cases a mixture of all these forms may be most convenient. Nor need the reader hesitate to repudiate with proper scorn all these suggestions as foolish and invent another method for his own use. It is even probable that he will be wise if he does so. For, just as the beginner should insist on his right to choose his own subject, so also he should endeavour to do his work in his own way.

Yet in case he should desire a little more consideration of this matter, a few more points may here be submitted for his acceptance or rejection. It has been said that the plan prepared should be clear and intelligible. It is not meant that it must be complete, and that nothing should be done until it is complete. A statement that on one or more portions of the subject nothing is known is clear and intelligible, though it possesses not even an elementary character of completeness. In fact much of the plan may well consist of such statements; and those parts must be left blank, until thought and new knowledge enable the student to fill them in. The point at which he should begin his systematic researches must be a point about which he knows something. But while he works at that part of his plan, he must carry the other parts in his mind; for as he makes notes for one part, he will come upon matter to be noted for other parts; and if he is not prepared for this, he will know the distasteful labour of going through material not once but many times in pursuit of the notes he needs for the whole of his research. There is then an inevitable conflict of method. The researcher cannot afford to limit his notes to a part of his subject; yet while he is making them, he will necessarily have one part more clearly present to his mind than the others. It is easy to state the difficulty, harder to point out the remedy. In fact a little thought will show that there is no remedy and that it is necessary to accept the difficulty, and fall back upon palliatives. Of these there are many to be found, and some may be suggested here, while the student will naturally discover many others for himself, arising out of the special character of the materials he is using.

The first of these palliatives will be found in an estimate of the number of notes he is likely to need. However careful he is he will certainly at first make more notes than he will use. Indeed, he will find himself compelled to do this, nor will the possession of a preliminary plan save him from this necessity. The very essence of his enquiry is not merely to substantiate the initial idea, but also to correct and enrich it; and it is always true that no one can take notes intelligently, until he knows the purpose for which they are needed, or know exactly what that purpose is, until the notes have been taken.

Yet as the enquiry proceeds, the investigator should gain a clearer view of the meaning of his original idea, and grow more sure of its value; and in the later stages of his work his notes will be fewer and more to the point.[1] For these reasons it is probably of little use to offer any numerical estimate of the amount of notes required for a particular research. But I will venture on this rather dangerous ground, well knowing that I am exposing myself to the peril of rebuke from those who are wiser than I am as well as from those whose criticism may be sharpened by inexperience. For a research, which resulted in an article of five thousand[2] words, I find I made between fifty and sixty notes and actually used in the article about twenty-five or rather fewer. It would have been easy to make ten times the number of notes and possible to give ten times the number of words to the subject. But on the whole I am not sure that the final result would have been improved by an increase in the number of notes, and it may well be doubted whether the subject was worth more words. It would not be true to say that the notes not used in the article need not have been made; in point of fact they had to be made simply to confirm the validity of the theory based

[1] The preceding sentences are due to a criticism made by Professor Becker.
[2] Further examination of this point convinces me that the number of notes required increases more rapidly than the number of words in the final statement. An article of ten thousand words will need more than double the number of notes required for one of five thousand words, and so on in an increasing ratio.

NOTES AND THE MAKING OF THEM 127

upon those that were used, and to supply the sense of conviction that this theory was properly founded, without which it would have been impossible to write clearly or definitely. With this explanation the foregoing estimate may be given as a fair average for a short research, and it may be taken that one note is amply sufficient for a hundred words in the finished work. Indeed, if any writer requires a larger proportion[1], it can only be because his mind is so unfurnished that he would be better employed in instructing himself rather than in endeavouring to instruct others. But to come back to the main point, the necessary number of notes; if these calculations are valid, the student should not expect that his whole store of material will be unwieldy. It will be seen later that there are many good reasons why he should take care that it is not.

Again, the collected notes will be of very varied length. An examination of the little collection on which these researches are founded shows that many of them are simply references needing only ten or eleven words. Some are even shorter—e.g., 'Sheriff's Case, Atkins, p. 248'. It may be objected that such a note errs on the side of brevity, and that in a year or two even the maker of it would hardly know what it

[1] To avoid misunderstanding let me repeat that these hints are intended for beginners. There are many inquiries in which large collections of notes are needed in order to understand the subject at all. But these are not questions that beginners should tackle.

meant, and that no one else could ever understand it. The latter part of the objection is irrelevant, because notes are made to be used by the maker and not by others; the first point is equally irrelevant, because the note was made merely as a reference to a particular book, lying ready to the maker's hand, and was meant to be incorporated in a complete shape in the article. It would have been waste of time to make it longer. But many of the notes are long and full. The longest runs to about three hundred and fifty words, and consists of a transcript of an entry on the Patent Roll of Henry IV, abbreviated by the omission of needless words. In the article it appears, but in a still more abbreviated shape. But it might easily have happened that it would have been discarded entirely. And so we reach another palliative, in the fact that many of the notes taken will be made for purely temporary use and may properly consist of a mere reference and a couple of words to explain their purpose.

It is true enough that these considerations are no remedy for the difficulty of taking notes on the whole subject, while the mind is directed only to a part of it; and they are not suggested as a remedy. All that they show, is that the whole mass of notes needed for a research need not be unwieldy, and that of that mass many notes will be brief, quickly made and only needed for temporary purposes. But the main difficulty remains and must be met. The two

NOTES AND THE MAKING OF THEM

weapons needed for dealing with it are a complete knowledge of the preliminary plan already mentioned, and a mind trained to seize any useful scrap of knowledge that may turn up by chance, even when the attention is not specially directed to it. An adventure, well known to me, may make the method clearer. Two friends and myself were engaged in a joint work, and in the course of it we found ourselves rather at a loss to understand the claim of the medieval earl to receive the third part of the judicial profits of his county. While engaged on an entirely different matter one of us happened to come upon some mention of a holder of fees in England, who went by the curious name of the Advocate of Béthune. Having met the name some scores of times before, he might easily have passed it by again with the slight discomfort one always feels at leaving unsolved some familiar puzzle. On this occasion by a lucky chance he determined that he would run the gentleman to earth and find out what he really was. A little search made it clear that his real name was Robert de Béthune and that he was also known as the Advocate of Arras. This did not seem quite satisfactory, and after some more digging, it finally appeared that Robert de Béthune was hereditary Advocate of the abbey of St Vast of Arras. By this time the curiosity of the enquirer was thoroughly inflamed and he meant to know even more about this advocate. As a first step he opened the glossary of Ducange at the word Advocatus; and there after noticing, what he already knew, that the advocate of an abbey was the man who presided over the courts held in the liberty of the abbey, he saw that by virtue of that office the advocate was entitled to a third share of all the money penalties paid in the courts held before him. The hereditary advocates of the abbey of St Vast and their English lands became of small importance in his eyes. The earl's third penny of the pleas of the shire swept from his mind French advocates and German vogts and the problem of their non-existence in England, and an investigation that began as an inquiry into the real name of a tenant-in-chief ended in a little bundle of notes on the proportion of pecuniary penalties due to the presiding judge.

This anecdote shows the importance of keeping the mind in an acquisitive mood, and the advantage of seizing a happy chance. From another point of view it is, however, a deplorable story. The investigation began well; the point aimed at was attained with a proper economy of effort. The next step was unnecessary, but excusable, though the proper course would have been merely to note that the exact nature of an advocate required further enquiry, and then return to the matter of the English fees of the Advocate of Béthune. But the last diversion was unpardonable. The whole question of the nature of an advocate was

NOTES AND THE MAKING OF THEM

dropped, and the mind of the student allowed to be turned on to another subject connected in no way with the main problem with which the story began. It is an adventure that could never have occurred to an investigator working on a logical system with a concentrated purpose directed by a definite plan. No adviser would be justified in telling a student to pursue such a course. Yet these happy chances, these unmerited rewards occur; and it is better to keep one's eyes open on all sides, rather than to keep them logically closed to all but one object. The real sin was that to this day that student is still ignorant of the reason why in England advocates and vogts did not exist.

From another point of view this incident deserves study. It shows that there are two methods of note-taking to be reckoned with, and each of those methods is appropriate for different ends. In fact the researcher will soon find that he has to deal with two classes of problems. In dealing with the first class he will require to work systematically through a book or a definite group of records, and extract in the form of notes everything that he may there find useful for his research. It is work needing in the highest degree patience, assiduity and concentration. Indeed the demand made for these qualities is so insistent, that in the exercise of them the worker is apt to forget that he cannot even here afford to work mechanically, though it is true that success requires many of the qualities of a machine. The student has before him, for example, a bundle of papers; one by one each must be picked up, examined, and its value discovered; some will be laid by as irrelevant, some must be abstracted more or less fully, some must be transcribed. Unless the worker can work without haste or rest, without interest almost, he will find the labour intolerably irksome and he may suffer sooner or later from that affliction of the beginner, the fatal suspicion that all his toil can bring no profit to himself or any other thinking man, and that the knowledge he is accumulating is either known already or not worth knowing. If that mood comes upon him, he will find upon reflection that his dejection is due for the most part to one error; he has tried to make his brain think out the ultimate value of every note he is making, while his attention is at strain to make them. He has not been enough of a machine. On the other hand it is easy to be too much of a machine; it is not difficult, for instance, to decide to transcribe a document in full, and to make the transcript and discover when it is complete that not the smallest fragment of the sense of the document has ever passed into thought. The attention has been there, the eye and the hand have worked perfectly together, but anything like thought or memory has been short-circuited. It is even possible to make an abstract of a complicated document in the same way. It might be supposed that such copies or abstracts would contain a large proportion of error; this is not the case. Errors there will certainly be in them, errors due to lack of critical insight, errors due to skipping from a word to the same word occurring in the next line below and others of the same kind. But on the whole the standard of accuracy will be as high as, or perhaps higher than, that attained by the man who as he copies or abstracts is thinking all the time how he can use his material, fitting each fact into its place in his theory and so interested in the object of his transcript that his attention wavers as he makes it. This man will makes as many errors or more, and his errors will be of a more flagrant kind. Neither way of work is of course the best. The ideal method is that of the worker who can use his attention and the direct relation of hand and eye to make his transcript or abstract mechanically and yet keep his critical powers and his observation on the watch to avoid error, and know what he is doing while he does it. The important thing is to limit the fatigue involved by excluding, as far as possible, all consideration of the final use of the notes made.

It may be said that this advice contradicts the whole of the advice previously given, since for work so done there is no need for a plan and indeed no room for the use of one. The answer to this criticism is not hard to find. The very object of the construction of a preliminary plan is to save the worker from the need of thinking out his plan while he makes his notes. His plan is to him what a map is to an explorer, a guide to tell him in which direction he should go, a warning of known difficulties, an indication of the unexplored tracts. With that plan he knows when he can go forward noting the details needed to fill in the half explored portions or to verify or correct the observations already made by himself or others. It is true that one object of the conscientious worker must always be to overthrow his own plan, and to reconstruct it anew. Indeed it is the peculiar privilege of all pioneers in research that they may derive almost as much pleasure from confuting their own theories or confirming those of others as they can from confirming their own guesses or confuting those of their fellow workers. At any moment an examination of a book or manuscript may produce some new fact destructive of the preliminary plan in whole or in part. The worker must be prepared for that, though if his plan has been wisely made, it will not happen even to the beginner as often as he may suppose. But the reconstruction of the plan or work in whole or even in part is not a task to be undertaken as an episode in the task of gathering notes, or even to be thought of at this stage. It is not even a reason for closing the book or documents with which the worker is engaged, and going away to think things over . It is merely a fact to be noted for future attention, when the task in hand has been carried through and the needful material for the alterations and repairs has been acquired. When that has been done, the revision of the plan can be considered, and in most cases it will be found that it is an extension of the plan rather than a new construction that will be necessary, or at the most an improvement of it. With each such extension and improvement the plan will grow in completeness; the unexplored tracts will diminish in size and importance and the plan will begin to look like a skeleton upon which the finished work may be built up. It will begin to consist less of questions whose answers are unknown and more of questions provided with satisfactory answers. And in this process lies the answer to the criticism with which this paragraph began. The original plan guides the researcher to the materials to be employed, and suggests the use to be made of them. The systematic exploration of those materials and the recording of the results of that examination in the form of notes follows next. The plan will require modification in consequence of the knowledge thus gained; and the two processes must go on side by side, but not simultaneously. Never, in short, break off the study of a mass of material, because the results seem to destroy the plan of research. Such a course will destroy the continuity of the work of taking notes, and damage the value of the collection. What is even worse, it may actually lead to error or waste of time. It is easy to over-value a single instance, to attach too much importance to one fact that will not fit into a generalized theory. It is possible that the supposed fact is wrong, and not the theory; it may even happen that there is no real incompatibility between the new fact and the theory. Before destroying or altering a plan of research on the strength of a single note, wait to see how many other instances of a similar kind are to be discovered. It happened once that some eager students came across a statement that the supply of ink to the Exchequer was the privilege of the sacristan of the *major ecclesia* of Westminster. They were working on a plan which contained the statement that at that date the Exchequer had its home at Winchester. They were also of opinion that the term *major ecclesia* meant a cathedral church. They then fell into two errors; they assumed that the fact overthrew the plan and tried to reconstruct it by removing the Exchequer to Westminster. When this theory was found to be impossible, they fell into worse ways and suggested that as Westminster Abbey was not a cathedral, it was necessary to correct Westminster into Winchester. A little less haste, a little more investigation would have revealed two further facts, that *major ecclesia* is sometimes used for any large abbey church, and that it was the sacristan of Westminster who sup-

NOTES AND THE MAKING OF THEM 137

plied the ink to the Exchequer even while the home of the Exchequer was at Winchester. The incompatibility of the new fact with the old plan was imaginary. It is well to complete investigations of the mass of material before revising the plan of research.

These remarks are only meant to lay down in the most general way the problems which anyone who is working through a definite mass of materials will have to solve. To deal with the particular problems presented by special kinds of materials it would be needful to discuss the materials themselves; and no effective discussion of this kind is possible without reference to the subject of the research undertaken. A few hints can however be added without passing on to this forbidden ground, forbidden because it is the deliberate purpose of this book to leave everything that relates to the subject itself in the hands of its owner. The most important of these hints will lead us at once into matter of controversy, the arrangement of notes when taken. At first sight there seems to be but one possible method, the use of slips of paper all of one size, which can easily be stowed away in boxes and classified in them for reference. The merits of this method are so clear that its disadvantages often escape notice; and it may even be admitted that when notes are being made not for the temporary purpose of one research but as an eternal memorial of the energy of the maker of them, no other method is possible. But where notes are being made for use by the maker with the clear intention of destroying them as soon as they have been exhausted, other considerations must be kept in view. The first of these is that a collection of notes made from one mass of material loses much of its meaning to the maker unless it is kept together in the order in which the notes were found and made; and the next is that, as has already been said, such notes will vary widely in size and importance. Both of these considerations suggest that the rule of a separate slip for each note is neither possible nor reasonable. The notes to be taken from one mass of material must be kept together because they have a common origin. They must be studied in the light of that common origin and subjected to a common principle of criticism. They must, as an aid to the memory, be kept in a compact form; it is not advisable to mix together for any scheme of classification, notes taken from masses of materials of different kinds.

All that has been said here applies only to the collection of notes on a large scale from large masses of materials. It was pointed out above that there was another method of note-taking to be considered. The student cannot always have the luck to deal with materials on a large scale. He will, only too often for his comfort, have to deal with small points. In particular he will have to deal with the troublesome business of identifying obscure places and people. Few tasks will put a harder strain on his ingenuity, or expose him to more serious risk of error. Take for example such a well-known person as John Mansell, the famous minister of Henry the Third. Nothing could seem simpler than to identify such a well-known man, wherever he appears. Unfortunately there were certainly two men of the name living at the same time, and it is indeed probable that there were even more[1]. This is no place to endeavour to unravel the windings of this maze or to attempt to explain the origin of the Master John Mansell, who witnesses a charter[2] of Philip de Ruylegh in favour of Sir John Mansell, the Treasurer of York. Now the chances are that any John Mansell whose name appears in a document in the reign of Henry the Third is the great John Mansell, but there is always the awkward chance that the unwary student may go wrong in this tangle. If, knowing of the trap, he embarks on the task of identifying a doubtful John Mansell, he will have to collect together a mass of notes, and his notes cannot be made in any other way than on separate slips. They will be taken from

[1] Somewhere—I think in the pages of *The Athenæum*—there is an article on the three John Mansells. Once I had a note of the reference. But that note is lost, and I cannot recover the reference. There is in *Notes and Queries* (February 1911, p. 191) an article by Mr. D. P. W. Mansell, which may be the lost authority. Any one who wishes to appreciate the confusion surrounding the whole matter may consult *The Family of Maunsel*, by Colonel C. A. Maunsel and Commander Statham, R.N., vol. i, p. 108 *seqq.* (Kegan Paul & Co.)

[2] *Calendar of Charter Rolls*, vol. ii, p. 8.

all sorts of sources, printed and unprinted, and the only link that unites them will be the name of John Mansell. There will be nothing else that the notes will have in common; no mere assiduity or mechanical accuracy will serve him; he will need all the luck he can deserve, and all the ingenuity he has. He will find that the estimate already given of one note to a hundred words of writing is a wild underestimate and that ten notes to one word of writing may be under the mark. This is of course an extreme case, a case where no one can be safe. But it is not an isolated case. Indeed, if any one would like another puzzle of the same kind, he need only endeavour to discover the christian name of the Huguenot captain de Mouy[1] who was assassinated by Maurevel the pensioned 'tueur du Roi'. From that problem he might go on to determine the exact relationship between the families of Vaudrey de Mouy and Vaudrey de St Phal, and so explain how Dumas in *La Reine Margot* came to call de Mouy, who revenged the death of his kinsman by killing Maurevel, Vaudrey de St Phal, a name which did not belong to him.

These are instances enough; the identification of places and persons is never an easy task. And there are other questions which require the same treatment. The meaning of obscure words, difficult dates, and all

---

[1] See *e.g.* Lavisse, *Histoire de France,* vol. vi, pt. 1, p. 126, for a starting point. There is more information to be had in the *Documents Inédits: Lettres de Catherine de Medici.*

the details of law and administration that may at any moment appear as new problems in the middle of an apparently straight-forward piece of work. It would be unreasonable to suggest that it is within the power of a beginner to deal with all such points; a few he may settle, more he must admit that he cannot settle. The thing for him to remember is that notes of these special points must be made on separate slips, and the slips arranged under the special points and not under the source from which they come. It is of course likely that among the notes collected from the various masses of material examined there may be some which bear on the special points. These must be left in the place where they belong, and if necessary a cross reference added to the special files.

There is one danger connected with these special investigations, which should not be left unnoticed. They should always be regarded as subordinate to the main line of investigation. It is only too easy to waste time and energy upon them. The work is difficult and interesting. It may easily become entrancing, and the beginner cannot expect to possess the wide knowledge of sources of information and the tactical skill needed for success. In particular he is apt to find himself entangled in nets of error prepared for him by the carelessness or recklessness of other enquirers. He must in every case decide for himself how far he will go in each case. But let him remember that he is always able to render service, and important service, by simply stating the problem and setting out clearly what he has tried to do and in what he has failed. Virgil in the *Georgics* declined to deal with the art of gardening. One line of his sums up the meaning of this paragraph:

Praetereo atque aliis post me memoranda relinquo.

It is one of the marks of a competent investigator that his work should suggest tasks for others to accomplish.

Before coming to the last section of this chapter there are a few loose threads to be cut off. It has been said that the investigator might find opportunities to take notes either for the benefit of others or for his own future use. To do the first he must know the subjects in which others are interested. To have this knowledge he must frequent their company and put their minds into relation with his own, and barter knowledge and ideas freely with them. Something has already been said on this point, but it cannot be said too often. One of the happiest results of such intercourse is the interchange of notes. It is not necessary or even advisable to wait for any accumulation of such notes before passing them on; as soon as may be convenient they should be handed to the man who can use them. When given, they are his, his to use, his to reject as useless, his to admire or despise; the only claim the giver has on the receiver

NOTES AND THE MAKING OF THEM 143

is that the gift should be received with a proper respect for the good-will which has led the maker of these notes to spend time on the needs of another. They are at best only a recommendation to the receiver to look at the source from which they are taken in the hope that he may find there something that he can use. They may be, they often are invaluable in this way; but it is very rarely that notes taken by one man are of immediate use to another.

The taking of notes for the future use of the taker is not an easy problem. One thing is clear; it is a temptation to stray from the main task and to waste time. On the other hand the neglect to make notes, when the chance is there, may seem in later years subject for repentance. Somewhere there exists a writ of prohibition issued by James I forbidding all ecclesiastical courts to hear any attack on the legality of a marriage between an uncle and a niece. It must be many years since I saw that writ. It amused me at the time, and I remembered the fact. But now I do not know who the uncle was or who the niece, or where I saw the writ. And thus when I wanted to mention it not long ago, I could not do it and I became aware that all that I really knew was that I had once known it. But if a note had been made at a time, when the maker could have no expectation of needing it, would it have survived? All sorts of chances might have put an end to it. Suppose it had by some good luck escaped moves, tidyings, the destruction of useless papers and been kept in safety among other casual notes, classified in a carefully arranged card index. Would the maker of it have been able to use it after all those years? The only answer that can be given to this question is this; that he could only have used it if he had remembered that he had made it. At the beginning of this chapter it was pointed out that a collection of notes was an extension of the memory. It may be added that it may easily become a means of laying an additional burthen on it. For my own part I will confess that I do not know whether I feel more humiliated by discovering that I have not made a note which I require, or by discovering that I have forgotten the existence of a note that I actually made. These are the two woes that await him who lays up notes for future use. The only consolation that can avail against them may be found in the reflection that after all no mechanical device for assisting the memory can replace it. Even the devout student of Paley's *Evidences,* who made an abstract of that work, and a synopsis of that abstract, and an abstract of the synopsis, and so continued until the whole marrow of the work was compressed on to one slip, found that he had wholly forgotten the wording of the slip at the moment when he most needed it. It is useless to provide aids for a memory which cannot remember the aids.

There is yet another point to be discussed, the nature of the notes themselves. On this little that will be of practical use can be said. Notes are an aid to the memory; their nature depends, therefore, on the memory that they are to aid, and on the purpose for which each note is made. Only the researcher himself can settle these points with any authority since he alone can know his own limitations and his own object. Two warnings may be given. Never make a trivial note, never in other words aid the memory to remember something that it ought never to forget or never to require to remember. A conscientious worker will actually make bibliographical notes on books familiar to him and all other students, and that without the least intention of printing the notes in his final work. He will even enshrine in a note his conviction that Madox's *History of the Exchequer* is difficult to use and fails to give information on many important points. All researchers, it may be admitted, make trivial notes of one kind or another, saving always those who by special inspiration never stray from the right path. The other warning, and quite as needful a warning, is this. Never make a note for future use in such a form that no one but yourself can understand it, and that even you yourself will not know what it means, when you come upon it some months later. This seems a trivial warning, one that no one, not the most foolish, could disobey. Yet such notes are made, and the odd thing is that the more notes a man has made, the more likely he is to make notes of this insufficient kind.

So far we have only considered notes taken from the materials upon which the contemplated work is meant to be based; there are, however, notes of another kind, which must be considered. These are the notes briefly mentioned above[1], the notes recording the mental processes of the worker, notes of the tentative conclusions, the fresh views, the half-seen truths, which arise in his mind as his work goes on; and to these we may perhaps add the notes of the happy phrases, the well-turned sentences, which arise half unconsciously in moments of meditation and inspiration. Now the making of all notes is only justified, when they are made as an aid to the memory, and when they record things worth remembering. If then, the student fears, and it is often a reasonable fear, that he may forget any of these things, and is quite sure that he wishes to remember them, let him note them down. The tentative conclusions, the fresh views, the half-seen truths will find their appropriate place in his plan of work, in the preliminary 'drama' of his subject, which will grow and be enriched by their inclusion. The statement of them must be full and clear, so full and clear that no doubt of their

---

[1] See p. 119 above. This discussion springs from a suggestion made to me by Professor Notestein.

meaning and value can ever remain in his mind, as he reads his notes. They should always be set down with all the point and style, which he has at his command, and supported by all the arguments, which commended them to his attention when he first thought of them. The notes need not be long, they should be as concise as possible; but they should be carefully written, and intended to enforce the attention of anyone who might read them, not merely capable of recalling a point to the mind of the man who made them. For this care there is good reason; they are meant to preserve the memory of a mental process, and nothing is so elusive as a mental process; nothing is easier to misinterpret, unless it is carefully recorded. Again all these happy accidents of study have their danger; the delight of their discovery blunts criticism; it is only by setting them down in full form that the discoverer can really judge whether they are worth making at all; and it is a saving of effort to test their worth as soon as possible.

The notes of happy phrases, and well-turned sentences are, *nisi fallor,* of very doubtful value. Some students seem to find them of use; they will keep a collection of such notes arranged in the order in which they intend to use them, and incorporate them in their pages as they write. Men work in many ways, and have every right to 'pursue happiness' as they think fit. But it may be suggested that these happy phrases, these well-turned sentences will too often turn out to be mere fleeting ghosts, informed with no intelligence and at the best only detached ornament, which it is difficult to use in the finished work. They cannot be tested as they stand alone; and it is scarcely possible to record them so fully as to show their worth or their uselessness.

There are many warnings in this discussion; and the ideal researcher needs none of them. All his notes will be to the point and all intelligible, complete and containing nothing superfluous, arranged so that he can find what he wants without putting any strain on his memory to remember where each note is. He will have made his plan of research, altered and improved it as he collected his notes, and so made it keep pace with his collections that the plan itself is a guide to them. If all this has been successfully carried out the plan will have become something not unlike an abstract of the final article. It might take the form of a continuous statement of the proposed divisions of the subject written on half-margin, with the references to the notes to be used entered on the margin. It might take half-a-dozen or more other shapes. But at any rate it will exist, it will have replaced the constructed drama described in the first chapter of this book, upon which indeed it may have originally been founded, and all the errors and ignorances of that preliminary sketch will have disappeared.

In all likelihood it will be lifeless, without the power to compel a reader's attention; it will certainly bear no relation to the general course of history, and may in all these qualities be much inferior to the constructed drama. But it will exist, and the next step which the researcher must take, is to endeavour to give to this plan and these collected notes all the qualities needed to make them something more than a mere collection of accurate statements covering many sheets of type-written paper.

V

THE FINAL STATEMENT

THERE are certain qualities that every reader has a right to ask from any work which he is invited to read; there are others for which he has a right to hope. The writer who desires to be read must endeavour to supply both qualities in as large a measure as his powers permit. Nor must he be deterred from doing so by the discovery which he will soon make, that the two sets of qualities are not wholly compatible, that it is not easy to combine completeness and accuracy with an easy and pleasant style of writing. Indeed he is likely enough to think that the second set of qualities are really in the nature of the carrot which may be used to tempt the donkey through its needful toil, and in that error he may fall into the blunder of acquiring a contempt for his reader. During the whole process of his research he has aimed at acquiring complete and accurate knowledge, he has collected detail after detail, piled proof on proof, made himself familiar with every issue and done all he could

THE FINAL STATEMENT

to economise his own efforts and enrich his own store. He is in a position to produce a complete and accurate statement in logical form, with the proper apparatus of bibliography, notes, documents, and the rest; these qualities the reader has a right to demand, and these he is prepared to give. In all he has done he has endeavoured to be a stern critic of his own doings; and he is willing to let his reader be an even sterner one on those lines. What more, he may ask with some asperity, ought he to have done? Is it expected that he 'should invest his work with literary merit'? Is he to write like Macaulay?

There is no reason why he should try to write like Macaulay or like any one else. There are many reasons why he should do nothing of the kind. A little study of Macaulay will readily produce some of them. There is a fine passage in Macaulay's history[1], in which he is describing the speech delivered by William III to the States of Holland when he was bidding them farewell before he started on his expedition to England. It ends with the following sentence:

"In all that grave senate there was none who could refrain from shedding tears. But the iron stoicism of William never gave way; and he stood among his weeping friends calm and austere, as if he had been about to leave them only for a short visit to his hunting grounds at Loo".

[1] Vol. I, p. 561 (Popular edition, 1889).

No one who reads can deny its value. And yet its value rests on an unsound foundation. As the words "grave senate" slipped from Macaulay's pen, his mind went back to Rome, and to the scene when Regulus made his farewell to the senate, and the famous passage from Horace[1] came to his mind. 'Torvus' became iron stoicism, 'interque moerentes amicos' was translated "among his weeping friends," and for the fields of Venafrum and Spartan Tarentum we have "his hunting grounds at Loo". But between Regulus and William there is no real likeness; and there is no likeness at all between their stories. The whole value of the passage rests upon a trick[2], and when the trick is once seen, it becomes, amusing indeed, but capable of impressing only those who do not discover it. But this criticism does not end the matter; it only shows a weakness in Macaulay's method, and passes over the real merit of the passage. If the parallel had been unassailable, every word in the sentence would have been enriched by the memories called up in the reader's mind. The words of Horace would have sounded in his ears as he read the words of Macaulay, and the two strains of thought have sounded together as the Marseillaise is half heard

---

[1] *Odes*, Book III, v. The passage is at the end of the ode.
[2] It is possible that Macaulay was himself unaware of the origin of the purple patch, and that he took the passage from Horace unconsciously. But this seems to me unlikely. It is more likely that he seized the chance to make the allusion and did not consider whether the suggested parallel was valid or not.

through the earlier stanzas of Schumann's setting of *The Two Grenadiers*.

But the beginner, who desires to imitate Macaulay, is more likely to imitate his failures than his successes. He will lack his retentive memory, his wide reading, his power of enforcing attention, and easily fall into the fatal snare of using rhetoric as a screen for poor logic and defective knowledge. Nor will he fare better if he chooses another model, or even tries to form a style by an eclectic study of many authors; he is more likely to capture their failings than their excellencies. His business should be not to write like others, but to write like himself. This, it may be thought, is an easy thing to do. It is really a great and difficult adventure, only to be accomplished slowly and in most cases imperfectly. He comes to his task of writing hampered by his accumulated notes, restrained by his natural diffidence. Like an unskilled general his movements are encumbered by his baggage and he has not the art of putting all his forces into battle array. He knows that if he tries to write well, he may easily write badly; he has often heard that easy writing means hard reading. It is only a natural consequence that he should fall back on a pedestrian style and confine himself to a mere reproduction of his notes, trusting rather to his facts than to his powers of expressing them. To all these difficulties may be added the magnitude of the task before him, the manual labour of the actual writing, the mental effort of using the right word and fitting the sentences into paragraphs and the paragraphs into chapters, without leaving too obvious gaps between the sentences, and only sufficient gaps between the paragraphs. Above all he must, as he writes, use all he knows, and use it in such a way that the main points shall stand out clearly, while at the same time the background, against which they are to show, is left neither unfilled nor yet intrusive.

Nevertheless a little experience will show that many of these difficulties are illusions, which disappear when attacked, and that the line of attack is not difficult to discover. It consists for the most part in a change of mood, in the adoption of a new point of view, in perceiving that in gathering the material for his work, he was occupied solely in furnishing his own mind, while in writing down his results his concern must be with the mind of his reader. The main source of errors in exposition is the failure to understand the mind of the reader[1], and it is the first task of a writer to learn to judge his own writing as he would judge that of another.[2] There are two obvious difficulties which he will have to overcome and a number of

---

[1] 'Pro captu lectoris habent sua fata libelli.' Most people know the latter half of the line; fewer remember the first three words, the most important part.

[2] See Sainte-Beuve's article on *Guillaume Favre* in *Causeries du Lundi*, vol. xiii, esp. p. 238, and the sentence: "Il ne se met jamais à la place de lecteur."

THE FINAL STATEMENT

others less obvious. Some of these he must be left to discover for himself because they will be the result of his own habit of mind, a peculiarity not suitable for general discussion. The first obvious difficulty is the natural disposition of the beginner to over-estimate the mental equipment and the power of attention of his reader. He will endeavour to write only for experts and examiners, and forget that even these luckless and criminal classes are human. An examiner is supposed to be able to discover the limits which divide the ignorance of a candidate from his knowledge; the task of a candidate is to tell the examiner all that he and the examiner know, and to avoid the subjects of which he himself is ignorant, while inserting in his work everything which he hopes will be new to the examiner. It is therefore likely that the beginner who thinks of the examiner as he writes will tend to fall into two errors. In the first place he will insert into his work everything that he ought to know, feeling that he must show that he knows it, and so produce in the reader, who is not an examiner, a sense that there is too much padding to be got through before he can come to the main points. Again, he will be reluctant to display his ignorance, since examiners are not prone to award marks for admissions of ignorance[1]; though in researches, an admission of ignorance by the writer will often be the

---

[1] I have heard that it is done, all the same.

very thing that the reader is looking for. On the other hand the writer who determines to write only for the expert hampers himself in other ways. He will be tempted to omit facts and comments that seem unworthy of submission to such great minds; he will exaggerate the knowledge of the expert and become obscure simply because he desires to avoid the danger of being common-place, and will therefore produce a work which no one but an expert can read and which even an expert will read reluctantly, if at all. Nor indeed are these the only misconceptions which may lead the writer astray. Sometimes he will be seized with a contempt for himself and for his reader alike, and fall into recklessness of bad writing out of mere despair. Or again his wish to enforce attention may lead him into a determination to shock his reader at all costs by exaggerations of style or matter or both, until under such treatment " Life becomes a Spasm, And History a Whiz "[1]. Sometimes this method succeeds, especially with the least instructed readers, and within limits it has its uses in compelling the reluctant reader to momentary attention. But like garlic in a salad, the moment it is noticed, it is apt to produce a complete rebellion in the reader, who only enjoys it as long as he does not perceive how he is being practised upon. With these methods may be

[1] *Phantasmagoria, and other Poems*, by Lewis Carroll, ed. 1911, p. 129, in " Poeta fit non nascitur."

THE FINAL STATEMENT

put the excessive use of paradox, especially of unexplained paradox, or the use of a magnificence of style not demanded by the matter in hand.[1] Nor can we pass over the possibility that in his endeavour to avoid a dry style, the writer may be tempted by devices of the journalist and so " fall into the jaws of Scylla while avoiding Charybdis ", which is a thoroughly absurd method of escaping from dryness.[2]

But it is time to return to the discussion of the remedies for these troubles; they may be summed up once more in a few sentences. Write to please yourself, as if you were to read what you are writing. Do your own criticizing as you go along. If you despair and desire to burn all you have written, select your kindest friend and ask her to read your work and tell you how it is getting on. Never destroy what you have written and begin over again, unless you are sure that you can do it better; and if you decide that this is necessary, use in the new version all that you can save in the old one. Remember that every time you rewrite what you have written you will lose something valuable, and therefore make quite sure

---

[1] *e.g.* " The bed is on the retiring principle. By means of swivels the whole paraphernalia of a *sanctum sanctorum* may be withdrawn from view, and the marchioness may receive the sons and daughters of fashion, clad in appropriate costume."—Mogg's edition of Paterson's *Road Book,* in the description of the Marquis of Exeter's state-bed at Burleigh House.

[2] See on all this *A Dictionary of Modern English Usage,* by Fowler and " Calloway's Code," by O. Henry, in *Whirligigs,* p. 48.

that you will gain more than you lose. To all this there is an important qualification to be added. There seem to be two ways of writing; in the first way the writer aims at attaining the final result right off; he thinks first and writes later. Revising is hateful to him, the mechanical toil of writing unpleasant. It is mainly for those who work in this way that these suggestions are made. But there is another way of writing which suits other minds better. They prefer to work like those artists who make a drawing by covering a sheet of paper with a network of pencil lines, from which they will then select the best, and after inking them in will remove those rejected.[1] A man who works in this way will double his paper down the middle, and work in the two columns thus formed. He will write his first draft in one column and keep the other for any additions that he may desire to make. He will strike out the portions he dislikes, interlineate, change words, insert new matter, and correct it; when he is at last content his manuscript will be a maze in appearance, an apparent wilderness, through which only its author or a careful copyist can find a way. Either method will create a good book; or any intermediate method. Each writer must work out his own method for himself; he alone can tell which will suit him best.

[1] Macaulay wrote in this way. He did not, however, use two columns. Of course a first draft may be made in any way. See *Life* (edition 1889, p. 501).

THE FINAL STATEMENT

There is one more general rule worth giving. Very few men can write well who have not read largely, not only historical works, but all kinds of prose and verse. It has been said that it is futile to adopt the style of another writer consciously. But a man's style is only in part the expression of his own intellectual character; it is influenced by the books he has read, and enriched not by the imitation but by the knowledge of the ways of other writers and the observation of their words and sentences. Nor should such reading be confined to one language. Historical students have a pestilent conviction in their minds, that they must know other languages in order to be able to read the books written in them which they need for their work. This is a monstrous misconception. They must know other languages in order to read them, and to read largely in them. A man, who learns French or German to read only specialist works written in those tongues, will find that he has gone through much toil and missed half his reward; he has missed the chance of improving his knowledge of his own language by becoming acquainted with the best ways of writing another. It must not be thought that during the progress of his research, and particularly during the writing of his final result, the worker has no need to find time for varied reading. While he writes, he needs most to read. In any book, worth calling a book, in any civilized language he will find passages that will show him how to add to his methods of expression. When his interest in his own work flags and his pen seems numb and his words lifeless, let him turn to a French book and see if he can discover the secret springs of the clarity and neatness achieved by the best French writers.[1] Others may find German books more useful. Some again will prefer to look for inspiration in their own language, fearing that they may fall too easily into the habit of writing in two languages at once. But whatever choice may be made, the rule should be observed, and on no consideration should the researcher totally abandon all general reading while he is engaged in his research or in writing out the results of it. For only by keeping a door open to all possible impressions can the beginner avoid the danger that research may dull his mind and destroy his imagination.

It is needless to say that this portion of the chapter is little more than a series of suggestions. Much is left to the reader's own intelligence and invention. The rest of the chapter is needed for the more important subject of the actual work of writing. The first point to be considered is the possible rate at which the writing can be done; and this rate is by no means a constant quantity. No two men write at the same rate, and no one writes at the same rate every day, or

---

[1] For my own part I find Saint-Beuve's *Causeries du Lundi* a good book to read while I write. But this is a matter of taste.

THE FINAL STATEMENT

on all subjects; and in consequence the following estimates are necessarily speculative.[1] Few writers can write for long at the rate of a thousand words a day if they wish to write carefully and with enjoyment; most can write three hundred words a day for an unlimited period. These limits are, of course, not meant to apply to practised writers, about whose powers it is difficult to form an opinion; they are the limits within which a beginner may expect to find his own output. The rate attainable depends on many things; it depends on the writer's manual skill with the pen, on the amount of time spent in settling what to say and how to say it; something must be allowed for looking up necessary references and consulting notes; above all it will depend on the extent of the writer's knowledge of the details and plan of his subject. On an average somewhere about six hundred words a day is a fair rate of progress for original composition. If we turn from the daily rate to the measurement of the total time, other difficulties will meet us; the total length of the book is unknown to anyone but the author; of that total length a part will consist of transcripts of original documents, which for the most part should have been prepared during the process of collecting materials. There should also be a stock of bibliographical notes and descriptions of documents only needing to be inserted in their proper

[1] I do not think anyone has ever studied this curious subject.

places. These possessions may easily raise the average rate over the whole book very considerably; but the amount of them will vary with the nature of the book, and vary within such wide limits that no estimate is possible that would be of any value. The only person who can make all these allowances is the writer himself; if he can do so with any accuracy, he can then make a guess at the total time he must give to his writing. All that can be said here is that in six months there are twenty-six weeks, and that any one who writes six hundred words a day for five days in each week will have written nearly eighty thousand words at the end of six months. Nor will he want to write any more for some time, when he has done it.

The actual time required to write this daily task is not great. It is not difficult to write carefully and legibly up to about twenty words in a minute, and fifteen is easy work; so that the actual writing of the whole six hundred words cannot need as much as one hour. If we treble that time to include some intervals for thought, we get a total working day of about three hours. Even the laziest worker will scarcely consider this a full working day; and an energetic worker will certainly object that, if he can write six hundred words in three hours, there is no possible reason why he should not work six and turn out twelve hundred words a day. No doubt he can, but only on condition that he has ready in his mind what he wishes to set down, and also that he can stand the heavy strain of writing six hours a day, on a difficult and complicated subject which can be only imperfectly present to his mind. If any one cares to try a conclusive experiment on the point, let him take a sheet of paper and write out on it for a given time some passage of prose or verse that he knows by heart. Next let him copy for the same time a passage from a book that he has never read before. Then for the same time let him write down an account of some historical event or discuss some difficult historical question with which he is familiar; and lastly let him try to deal with a matter of which he has not previously thought. Finally let him examine his output; the result, if fairly tried, will convince him that the power of writing quickly and without strain simply depends on the amount of thought that must be given to what is being written, while the writing is being done. If, therefore, the rate of writing is to be increased, this can be done only by shaping the matter in the mind of the writer so perfectly that he can write straight out of his mind. To be able to do this he will need to have a complete mastery of his materials, and he will need to know the plan of his book, to know the plan of the whole book in outline, and the plan of the chapter at which he is working in detail, and the plan of the section in which he happens to be as definitely as may be possible.

If at this point the reader will recall what he has read in these pages, he will remember that he was advised to begin by constructing a 'drama' of his proposed work. As a little consideration will show, this drama is really a plan of the book. In its first form it is not likely to be a complete plan or even a correct plan, and one of the things that the writer has to do is to make it both complete and correct. In particular he must make it true to scale, and settle what fraction of the total space is to be assigned to each part of the subject. To do this he must examine his plan of research, the plan he was advised to make and keep by him while making his collection of notes. As the collection of notes grows, this plan will gradually become more and more complete, until in its final form it will have become a skeleton on which the whole book can be built up. With this skeleton and the collection of notes, the task of completing the final statement can be begun. The plan will, of course, determine the size of the book, and the relative scale of the different parts of it, more or less perfectly; but only the actual process of composition can finally fix the proper form of the whole book and its parts. To do this effectively the writer must keep a rough running account of the number of words he is using on each part of the subject. He need not know to a single word how many words are on each page of his manuscript, but he must know this within some limit of accuracy. If he writes with fair regularity and with but few corrections and alterations, it is easy to discover the average number of words that go to a page. If he adopts the method of writing and correcting as he writes, roughly hewing out his work and polishing and completing it sentence by sentence, he will find the discovery of an average more difficult. If he adds to this a habit of putting a widely differing number of words in each line, and a differing number of lines on each page, he may make it almost impossible for himself or any one else to know how much he is writing until a fair copy has been made. But, whatever difficulty may stand in the way, the writer who does not know how much he is writing is storing up trouble for himself and for others also. Nor is it specially the weakness of a beginner; there are not a few practised and experienced writers prone to this sin. To those who give much, much must be forgiven. But a beginner can scarcely demand such consideration, and for his own sake he ought to endeavour to acquire a habit of writing which will make it needless to require it.

When the size of the book and its parts has been determined, however roughly, the writer is ready for the next step, the actual composition. For this purpose he must begin by looking over his plan and his notes; he must read them through, arrange them, re-arrange them, play with them, criticize them, get them into his head, and then put them away out of reach before he begins to write. It is quite certain that a man who cannot write without his notes and materials before him, cannot write at all. He cannot write because he does not know what it is that he has to write. At the same time no man can possibly carry in his head all the materials for a book, not even for a short book. How much he can master at a time will depend upon his memory, his power of concentration and the speed at which he can work. All these factors differ in different men, and no estimate of them can be of any value. The more he can master at one time, the better for him; but it is a mere waste of time to try to overburden himself and overstrain his powers. He must, therefore, write as soon as he is prepared. On a previous page there is an estimate of the average amount that can be written in a day; here a warning may be added that that estimate is only a guess, and that a beginner may find it too high, or if he is lucky may find it too low. Each writer must fix the possible quantity for himself; and as soon as he has got that quantity shaped in his mind he must write it down, not using his notes or anything that he has written before, but relying on the new and fresh conception of it that he has just formed for himself. The creation of this conception needs steady and persistent thought, but

THE FINAL STATEMENT

even that preparatory thought will not be enough in itself, or at any rate not always. Sometimes and for some minds, it is true, the mental conception may be so complete and accurate that the mere writing is little more than a mechanical task; and the words can be set down by the pen with little more effort than would be needed to copy from another manuscript. The pen is content with what it writes.[1] But more often the process of writing leads to criticism. The eye as it follows the words is critical, even the hand seems to object to the suggestions of the brain. The ear too has its part; the sentences may sound weak and shapeless; and the writer, as he sees, feels and listens to what he writes, grows to think that this at any rate will never do.[2] Then the mechanical process of writing ceases to be mechanical and becomes a task of reconceiving and recasting what is to be written in the act of writing it. The only thing to be done is to let self-criticism have its way, and to abandon

---

[1] There is a kind of rhythm or measure, an ordered movement, about all good or tolerable writing, which is appropriate to any particular subject or to the treatment of any part of it. Narrative and argument run to different measures; and the beat of an ironical passage differs from that used to express conviction. The author should have running in his head as he writes the proper measure, and see that the words fall into it as he writes. If they do not, there will be no pleasure in the process or the result.

[2] In some cases these difficulties come from the desire of a young writer to make every sentence an accurate statement in itself. The result is that he inserts into each sentence all the qualifying and explanatory clauses needed to make it exact. He will save himself much trouble by putting his definite statement in one sentence and adding his qualifying statements in others.

the previous conception and trust to the inspiration that actual writing brings with it. The preliminary work will not have been lost, and the final result will often be much better than the mental draft of it.

One thing will now become clear; there is no reason for leaving the whole task of writing out the final statement to be done at the end of the research. Too often the beginner falls into this trap. He fears that even when he has accumulated a sufficient supply of notes to write on one part of his subject, there may yet remain something undiscovered, some new find which may alter the whole view at which he arrived before that new document came to his hands. Let him reassure himself; such cases are rare. It is likely enough that he may unexpectedly come upon a find which will mean the insertion of a paragraph, the qualification of a statement, the cancelling of a page. But if his plan of research has been wisely made, if the exploration of his materials has been systematically done, it is not probable that any fresh fact will come to light of sufficient importance to upset his original conclusion completely. There is good reason for this assurance; the principal materials for most of the subordinate sections of a book will be found to occur in a few groups, and are not likely to be scattered among all the documents and books to be examined. The worker after some experience will find himself

THE FINAL STATEMENT

able to form a correct estimate on this point, and will know which sections must be left to be written last, and which can safely be attacked at any earlier stage. He may of course blunder in his estimate, and if he does he will have to revise what he has written. But the mere chance of this little disaster should not be allowed much weight compared with the great advantage that comes from writing with the materials fresh in one's mind, not to mention the escape from the terrible task involved in leaving the whole work of composition to be done at the last. Even of greater importance is another argument. The beginner is only too apt to fall under the charm of pure research, the delight of reading book after book on the same subject, of turning over document after document, of adding note to note, of constructing theory after theory. He feels that this is the true path for the scientific historian, that nothing he can write can ever be as beautiful as his researches, that the live facts which he has seen and handled will be dead when written down and that beside the researcher the writer is an inferior being. He puts off the ungracious task as long as he can. He 'leaves time to dogs and apes' confident in his possession of eternity. Sometimes the book is never written; the foundations are complete, the bricks are gathered, but the edifice is never raised. Sometimes the necessity of completing a hateful duty has to be faced at last, and the work is done against time, done somehow, done without art and without enjoyment.

Now it may be said that this method of writing a book in detached parts will result in a loss of unity, and that any book so written will be a collection of detached essays, and not a consistent whole. The danger certainly exists, and it is true that many works founded on careful research are open to this criticism. In dealing with some subjects it cannot be avoided; there is no real unity in the subject and it is useless to endeavour to conceal that fact. In his history of the Peninsular War, Napier almost succeeded in giving to that confused subject an artificial unity by adopting an epic treatment. But to do this he has to select first one character as his hero and then another; he has to introduce many episodes which break the current of his main narrative; and he has to throw into the background much of the story in order to leave the stage free for his principal characters. The result is a magnificent work of art; but the apparent unity is enforced on the reader by that art alone. Other writers have preferred to admit the essential lack of unity in their subject, and have openly divided their work into sections; they have treated the subject geographically, for instance, and relied upon a general introduction or special chapters to make the reader understand the connexion between the different portions of their work. This method is easy for the writer and, if he is able to avoid repeating the same explanations and comments in each section, it helps the reader to master the details of a complicated subject. Its danger lies in the possibility that an untrained reader will fail to discover in the detached sections, with their mass of detail, the reasons for the general principles set out in the chapters, in which the subject is dealt with as a whole. Nevertheless the method is often effective, because it gives opportunities for the careful treatment of details and allows the writer to deal separately with the more difficult task of explaining the general unity of his subject.

In the case of complex subjects, therefore, the beginner need not hesitate to write his book in detached parts. He may accept the loss of unity, and rely on his introduction or on special chapters to explain the general principles which he seeks to establish, and find there his opportunity to make his book into a consistent whole. But it may still be argued that this method of work is inadmissible where the subject is not complex, but simple and possessed of a natural unity; and the argument may be pressed further. It may be said that for the beginner at any rate it is unwise to select any subjects that are not simple, and that with such subjects it is only by doing all his writing in one effort, that the beginner can hope to produce a consistent whole. To answer this it will be necessary to consider the fundamental difficulty of narrative, and the relation between narrative and the events which it expresses. This difficulty consists in the fact that all narrative is effected by arranging words in a single line; and unless the events to be expressed also occur one after the other, they cannot be arranged in that manner. Further consideration will show that this last condition rarely exists. Events are not themselves simple points, but are only artificial units, formed by including under one term a number of details. As soon as these details are observed, the details become themselves events, and the process of analysis begins once more. With every such step the simplicity of the subject vanishes and the complicated truth appears. And so we reach the conclusion that to describe historical events in the form of a simple narrative is a task requiring the highest powers of art. The writer must be able to work on the lines of Paul-Louis Courier, who took for his motto "Peu de matière et beaucoup d'art". But Courier disliked and despised history, which he regarded as a succession of stupidities and atrocities; and his motto is one to be remembered rather than obeyed. To-day we must reverse his motto, and write in our note books "Much material, little art". But while we do this, it may be as well to keep in our inmost soul the conscience that after all Courier may be right. Sooner or later we may hope to reach the point where we can forget our

THE FINAL STATEMENT

notes and yet write with art and accuracy combined.[1]

But if it must be admitted that no subject is really simple, and that any appearance of simplicity is the result of the writer's art, it follows that the distinction between simple and complex subjects is a matter of degree, and that many subjects can be made to belong to either class by the kind of treatment adopted by the writer. In fact the writer must himself decide whether he will use the method of detached chapters already described, or whether he will undertake to set out the results of his reseach as a whole. Let us assume that he chooses the latter course, and attempt to explain how he should then proceed, and how he can still contrive to write his book, as he researches, without losing the unity of treatment at which he aims. To do this he must possess himself of so strong a conception of the main line of his argument, that it will always be present in his mind as he writes; he must have clear in his mind the plan of his book, and that plan must have been made with the intention of writing his book as a whole. That plan will be the main thread on which all the parts separately written can be finally strung. The thread cannot be purely chronological; it must also be rational. It must be linked together by logical argument in such a manner

[1] Courier doubted this; his opinion is that 'La science et l'éloquence sont peut-être incompatibles;' and his opinions are worth noting because he is a master of expression. I take this quotation from Sainte-Beuve's *Causeries du Lundi*, vol. vi, p. 329. Compare George Louis Beer's remarks in the preface to *The Old Colonial System*, vol. i, p. xii.

that the reader can see and follow the progress of the writer's thought; and the rational coherence must be expressed in the unity of style or tone used by the writer. If this conception has been thought out in the writer's mind and is always present in it, as he writes the detached portions, they will fall into their proper places, and though written separately will finally appear as parts of a consistent whole. It will happen of necessity that in some cases portions of the book must be treated as episodes. The main thread will not always be simple; it may split into two or three strands, which may re-unite again or may come to independent conclusions. These will form digressions from the main thread; in dealing with them the writer must definitely mark the point of divergence and the point at which they close. Some of the pages written separately may have to be strung on these subordinate threads; and it may even happen that there are cases in which there is no obvious place in which a particular bit of writing can be placed. In this case the writer must consider whether the difficulty is not really due to the fact that he has departed widely from the plan of his book, and simply wasted time on a subordinate subject which he need not have touched for his main purpose. If he comes to the conclusion that this is the case, he will do well to put aside that portion for future use. It may, however, be the case that such a course would impair his main argument, and that the information is useful as a collateral illustration or a supporting argument; and then the right course is to meet the difficulty by using that portion, placing it apart from the main treatise as an appendix or excursus. This should always be done where the matter consists of minute critical examination of doubtful documents, or careful discussion of controversial points.

It will be seen that the possibility of writing a book as a consistent whole and yet writing each part as the research needed for it is completed, depends on the construction of a preliminary plan. If the reader will now look back to the pages of the preceding chapters, he will see that the conception of such a plan is insisted on throughout, even at the cost of wearying the reader by over-repetition. The early shaping of such a plan must be imperfect, may even be mistaken; and during the process of research reconstruction and correction are inevitable. There will always be a preliminary stage when the student will have to look for his subject or force his subject to look for him. In some cases this stage may last far beyond the period assigned to it in this book, and during that stage the formation of a plan is impossible. Even when the subject and the student have met there may still be difficulties to be overcome; but the plan of research should be always kept in mind, and the plan of the book should be made to grow out of it. In carrying out this policy, much will depend on the contents of the worker's mind. Even if he is bent on keeping his work to the strictest form of monograph, and for that purpose intends to limit his mind and his thoughts to the narrowest conception of his subject, he will find that his control of his chosen field will depend on his general knowledge of history and literature and his power of forming and expressing general ideas. These qualities of mind cannot be improvised, they must have been prepared and acquired in the years that went by before the student began his work of research. The wider his education has been, the larger his interests, the better are his prospects of success. The less he has been taught, the more he has learnt for himself, the more likely he will be to succeed in forming his plan, and expressing it artistically and thoughtfully. There are those who will discuss whether history is a science or an art; the question is a vain one. Any attempt to construct a valid theory of observed facts rests on scientific principles; any expression of that theory is ruled by the principles of art. No book, not even a mathematical book, can be written without art; and in fact the art required to write a mathematical book is probably of a far more subtle and delicate kind than that required for the statement of the results of any other form of research.

Now it is probable that at this point the reader will

begin to think that for success in historical writing he must possess aptitudes and qualifications which few men, if any, can hope to acquire. This is an illusion, an illusion produced partly by the nature of the subject here discussed, and partly by the method of exposition adopted. Let us suppose that a man who had never walked and who was about to begin to walk, should be presented with a treatise on walking in which all the mechanism of balance, of the action of the muscles and joints, and of the means of preserving the intended direction of motion was described in detail. It would not be surprising if after reading it, the learner should pronounce that walking was impossible, for him at any rate, and that he would abandon the attempt to learn how to do it. The answer would be 'you cannot learn how it is done until you have learnt to do it'. The same answer is applicable here. The beginner who reads this book should remember that most of the difficulties here mentioned will disappear as soon as he discovers their existence; and that as his experience increases, his fear of them will diminish. He has already been advised to work among others doing the same kind of work and warned against the danger of solitary endeavour, as well as advised that he must to some extent face his task alone. Just as the man who learns to walk will find that for his first steps he will need the support of those experienced in that art, so in early days the advice of those experienced in research will save the beginner many a stumble and much discouragement. Such assistance he should ask for and use, but not rely upon. Such assistance the guide should give, give in the measure required, and be ready to withdraw at the right moment. There are, I am aware, passages in this book which may seem to insist too much on the necessity of independence in the student, and to assign too limited a sphere to the teacher. It is possible that this criticism may be valid; one who is neither a teacher nor a student may not venture to say when a teacher should cease to offer help and a student refuse to request it. If any passages in this book seem to be guilty of such presumption, let me at least on the last page end by saying that in my opinion the best guides are those who are always ready to give instruction and assistance, and that the best students are those who never need either. Wise teachers and wise students know how to escape from this antinomy; their method of escape is their own secret, and that secret they keep.

THE END